To Andy & Elana —

We praise God for
your friendship!

Happy Hanukkah!

Marilee Dunker

—1987—

A
BRAVER
SONG TO SING

MARILEE DUNKER

Zondervan Books
Zondervan Publishing House
Grand Rapids, Michigan

A Braver Song to Sing
Copyright © 1987 by Marilee Dunker

Zondervan Books
are published by Zondervan Publishing House
1415 Lake Drive, S.E.
Grand Rapids, MI 49506

Library of Congress Cataloging in Publication Data

Dunker, Marilee Pierce.
A braver song to sing.

1. Baltz, Patricia. 2. Christian biography—United States. 3. Christian
life—1960– . 4. Heart—Valves—Diseases—Patients—United States—
Biography. I. Title.
BR1725.B334D86   1987   248.8'6'0924   [B]   87-16216
ISBN 0-310-37591-6

Printed in the United States of America

87 88 89 90 91 92 / EP / 10 9 8 7 6 5 4 3 2 1

Thy servant, Lord, hath nothing in the house.
Not even one small pot of common oil
For he who never cometh but to spoil
Hath raided my poor house again, again,
That ruthless strong man armed, whom men call Pain.

I thought that I had courage in the house
And patience to be quiet and endure
And sometimes happy songs, now I am sure
Thy servant truly hath not anything
And see, my songbird hath a broken wing.

"My servant, I have come into the house—
I who know Pain's extremity so well
That there can never be the need to tell
His power to make the flesh and spirit quail.
Have I not felt the scourge, the thorn, the nail?

"And I, his Conqueror, am in the house.
Let not your heart be troubled, do not fear.
Why shouldst thou, child of Mine, if I am here?
My touch will heal thy songbird's broken wing
And he shall have a braver song to sing."

AMY CARMICHAEL

I

Since I've gone to the hospital to get a new part
That the doctors will put on the inside of my heart
I sat down and made up this new book for you
To look at, to laugh at, to read through and through.
While I am away and can't kiss you good night,
Or read you a story, then turn out the light,
You may find that you miss me, and feel a bit sad—
Then just open this book and I hope you'll be glad!

IT WAS LATE. The grandfather clock ticked out the seconds like the beat of a heart. The sound was familiar and comforting as Pann put the final touches on the notebook she had put together for her son. She had seen the small, inexpensive book at the local five-and-dime and had chosen it because the cover looked like faded denim, with a pocket stenciled on the front. It looked like a little boy's book, and K.C. was all boy—full of energy and life. And he was so bright. Everyone said he was an extraordinary four-year-old.

Pann slowly turned the pages and studied each picture she had chosen to illustrate her poem. Each page held a memory: a trip to Disneyland; K.C. in his Halloween costume; Bill and K.C. stuffing themselves with brownies on the Fourth of July; Christmas; Easter; and simple things like playing ball and good-night kisses.

The title page read *A K.C. Book* in bold red letters. The second page was a picture cut from an old Valentine. A little boy, much like her own, fair-haired and smiling, was riding a skateboard and holding a heart that said, "I love you." Pann had added, "To K.C. Love, Mommy."

On the next page she had pasted a picture of a bushy-maned lion that was squeezed into a hospital bed, a thermometer drooping from his mouth. "Since I've gone to the hospital . . . ," the poem began.

That about sums up the past few years, Pann thought. Four years of strokes, tests, operations, complications, and rehabilitation had left little time to be a wife or a mother—or anything else, for that matter. Now there was one more hurdle: open-heart surgery to replace the valve the doctors believed was causing her problems. She thought, *A little flap of skin, no bigger than a thumbnail, doesn't do its job, and the world turns topsy-turvy.*

Pann continued to flip through the book. She ached when she came to a photo of K.C. at two; it showed him waist-deep in a bath full of bubbles, looking like a happy baby on a television commercial. Oh, how she wanted to keep the memories alive, to make him know how much she loved him! Suddenly the little book seemed so important, its worth beyond price. *But if something were to happen, would it be enough?*

Pann felt the fear in the pit of her stomach as she thought about what lay ahead. "Oh, God," she whispered. Her words were little more than a soft rush of wind escaping from the metal throat tube through which she breathed. "Please give me a chance to give K.C. more than this little book. He needs me. Bill needs me. Your Word says You will give us a new heart. All I need is a new valve. Please give me the strength. Please!"

Pann sat quietly for a few minutes and scanned the room. It was cozy. The big Spanish-style fireplace was perfect for roasting marshmallows and making popcorn. It was a real *family* room. But she and Bill and K.C. had spent very little time together in it.

Why had God allowed the torment of the last four years? What purpose could there be in permitting a twenty-five-year-old woman, with a new baby and a husband who needed her, to suffer not just one stroke, but stroke after stroke after stroke? Hadn't she and Bill always sought to please Him, to be the kind of people He wanted them to be? They had done their best to keep their end of the bargain. Why hadn't He kept His?

Pann's eyes fell on a wall plaque. On it was written the Scripture that she and Bill had claimed shortly after their nightmare began: "I know the plans I have for you, says the Lord. They are plans for good and not for evil, to give you a future and a hope" (Jeremiah 29:11 LB).

Right now, open-heart surgery was Pann's last hope, and the future was something she dared not contemplate. Only the past was certain—a crazy mix of happy times she fought to remember and painful times she prayed to forget.

"Pann?"

She looked up. Bill, who had been watching her, was standing in the doorway. *What a nice-looking man*, she thought, *tall and slender, with strong, well-defined features and intense blue eyes*. His eyes had been one of the things that first attracted her. She was glad that K.C. had inherited them.

Those eyes looked at her now with a tense, questioning gaze, checking to see how she was. "Come on, Mouse. Come to bed. You've got a big day tomorrow. You've got to sleep."

Leaving her crutches by the couch, Pann rose unsteadily to her feet. She paused until the blood stopped pounding in her head; these days, even the simplest movements were an effort. "Decrepit at twenty-nine!" Pann laughed.

"Decrepit, but cute," Bill teased. He put a steadying arm around his wife, and together they walked the long hall to their bedroom.

Pann slept in exhausted spurts, tossing and turning as she tried to escape the thoughts that flickered, like images in a silent movie, through her mind. There had been so much preparation for her hospitalization, so much to think about. Who would take care of K.C.? Who would take care of *her* when she came home? What if she came home permanently disabled—or not at all? She and Bill had spent hours discussing the possibilities in quiet, reasonable voices, the way one might talk about stock options or any other risky venture. It was the mature thing to do, necessary—and totally terrifying. Pann had signed her will with a combination of relief and foreboding. Decisions had been made; plans of action had been decided upon for every eventuality. Life would go on—with or without her. There was nothing left to do but wait.

Finally the morning came. The air had the crisp, clean bite of early January, and the sky stretched out like a painter's canvas, graduating in color from a deep rose to the palest of blues. It promised to be a classic California day.

Early morning had always been one of Pann's favorite times. She never got over the joy of waking up in her own bed to find Bill beside her. Leaning over, she gave him a wake-up kiss, then slipped out of bed and made her way to the kitchen to start the coffee. When the coffee was ready, Pann poured two steaming mugs and took one to Bill as he shaved in the bathroom; then she went back to the kitchen to set out K.C.'s cereal and make two sack lunches.

Business as usual, thought Pann as she spread peanut butter on a slice of bread for K.C. and wrapped cold chicken for Bill. After packing the lunches, she grabbed a couple of napkins. She stuffed one napkin in K.C.'s bag. Then she took a pen and drew a large heart on the other. "Pann loves Bill and always will," she wrote on the inside. At the bottom, she deftly drew a picture of a mouse and added several *XXX*'s and *OOO*'s for good measure.

"Morning, Mommy," said a husky little voice.

Pann turned to see a small disheveled figure rubbing the sleep out of his eyes. "Morning, Sweetie. Sit down and eat. Phyllis will be here to get you before too long."

"Great!" said K.C. with enthusiasm. He enjoyed visiting his "other families." After all, he was the guest of honor and always got royal treatment from those who volunteered to care for him during Pann's hospital stays.

Bill hurried into the kitchen as he gulped down the last of his coffee. "I gotta go. Bye, Buddy," he said, giving K.C.'s head an affectionate ruffle. "See ya later. Be good, ya hear?"

"Sure, Buddy," answered K.C., with the same inflection. "Don't worry about me."

Pann smiled at her two men. They were alike in so many ways. Having spent so much time together during her hospitalizations made them more than just father and son; they were friends, with a deep relationship that she sometimes envied.

Pann walked to the door with Bill. "You're sure you're all right?" he asked. "I hate not being able to drive you to the hospital myself, but nothing much is going to happen today; I'd rather take the time off later—when you really need me."

"I'll be fine. I've checked into so many hospitals, I could do it in my sleep." Pann gave him a reassuring hug. "Have a good day, and I'll see you tonight."

Despite her display of confidence, Pann's spirits drooped as Bill's car pulled from view. But before the feeling could overwhelm her, she thought of K.C. and knew she could not let go. Not yet. Besides, she hadn't given him his book yet.

Pann got the book and sat down at the table, where her son was downing his second bowl of cereal. "I've got a present for you."

K.C.'s eyes lit up at the sight of the little book. "K.C.! It says, 'K.C.'!"

"That's right," said Pann. "It's your very own book, all about you and me and Daddy and all the things we've done and the people we love. I thought it would cheer you up while I'm gone."

"Thanks, Mommy! Will you read it to me?"

"Not now. I think you ought to save it. It'll give you something to look forward to. It's my way of keeping you company, even though I can't be with you. Okay?"

"Okay." K.C. was silent for a moment, then looked up and asked, "Mommy, after your operation will your whisper be gone?"

The question took Pann off guard. She looked at her son's earnest expression. *Oh, Lord,* she thought, *what do I say?* Since her third tracheotomy tube had been implanted, Pann had been unable to talk above a whisper. Her vocal cords were paralyzed, and the doctors doubted that they would ever recover. For several months, she had communicated in a low, husky whisper, which made telephone conversations frustrating and had forced her to blow a whistle to call for her son or husband. It was hard for all of them, but Pann had not been aware of how deeply it affected K.C.

"Honey, I'm going to the hospital to get my heart fixed, not my voice," Pann answered gently. "It probably won't make any difference."

"Oh." K.C.'s whole body seemed to sag. Suddenly he flashed one of his dazzling smiles. "But it could. It could make a difference if Jesus wants it to! We'll just have to wait and see!"

"Oh, K.C.!" Pann laughed, grabbing him to her in a big hug.

Saying good-bye to her son that morning was one of the hardest things Pann had ever done. As she watched him march out to Phyllis's car, lugging the suitcase he insisted he could carry himself, she fought desperately against the thought that she might not see him again—or hold him or kiss him or have the joy of watching him grow up. As she stood waving after the car, throwing kisses to the little face flattened against the back window, she thought her heart was going to break.

Too late, said a wry little voice in her head. *It's already broken.*

Finally the tears came.

II

CHECKING INTO Cedar-Sinai Hospital in Los Angeles is like entering another world. Its U-shaped edifices cover an entire city block and stand eight stories high. But even more overwhelming than its size is the sense of importance and purpose you feel when you pass through its doors. Some of the most brilliant minds in modern medicine are associated with Cedars. It is a center of learning where new thoughts and experimentation charge the air with the excitement of unlimited possibilities.

The clock in the lobby read two o'clock that Thursday afternoon as Pann checked into the open-heart unit on the sixth floor. A friend from her Bible study, Sharon Davis, had kindly offered to drive her to the hospital and help her through the tedious registration procedure.

Stepping off the elevator on the sixth floor, Pann felt as if she was entering an elite hotel instead of a hospital. No bare linoleum floors or medicinal smells greeted her. The large, open waiting room was tastefully decorated in earth tones, with comfortable chairs and couches grouped around to give families separate areas in which to gather while their loved ones were in surgery. The walls throughout the hospital displayed a colorful collection of modern art prints, and the outside walls were massive expanses of glass through which the busy streets of Los Angeles could be observed. The overall feeling was one of positiveness and caring. Cedars was not a place where people came to be sick. It was where they came to get well.

Pann felt a cautious optimism as she and Sharon walked the long hall to her room. Every time she thought about the miraculous events that had brought her here, she remembered Jeremiah 29:11: "'I know the plans I have for you,' declares the Lord." Surely this must be a part of the plan.

Of course there are some things that don't change from hospital to hospital, and Cedars was no exception. Pann gave out a little groan as she entered her room and spotted the standard hospital gown neatly folded on the bed.

"The notorious backless wonder!" she said, rolling her eyes in disgust.

"Come on," said Sharon, fighting to keep a straight face, "I think it's kind of cute. Anyway, it's certainly practical."

"Yeah. One size fits all!"

As Pann slipped into the gown, she couldn't help thinking how much time she had spent in one of these drab, shapeless garments.

"Oh, well," said Sharon, as if reading her thoughts, "think of all the money you've saved on fashions that are in today and out tomorrow."

"You're right," Pann answered dryly. "If I time this right, all my old clothes will be back in style."

Both women laughed and continued chatting easily while

Sharon helped Pann put her things away. She left just as a young male nurse named Paul came in to officially welcome Pann to Cedars by popping a thermometer in her mouth and taking her blood pressure. Pann liked Paul immediately. She was grateful for his friendly conversation and gentle manner as he went through the necessary medical checks. He seemed to care about her as a person, something Pann had come to appreciate deeply. There had been times in the past when the nurses seemed to forget they were dealing with a human being rather than a "stroke in room ten" who needed her IV checked or her bedpan emptied.

After Paul left, Pann lay on the bed and willed her heart to stop racing. The last few months her heart rate had been dangerously high, causing her to feel weak-kneed and light-headed. Occasionally she would black out entirely, waking to find herself sprawled on the floor in an unladylike heap. Only a few weeks before, she had fainted in the kitchen, gashing her leg on the table. She awoke in a pool of blood and had to go to the emergency room to have her leg sutured. But even more disturbing than the blackout was the fact that no one seemed able to help her. She had had every test in the book, and still no answers had been found.

It was during this time that a chance call put Pann in contact with Dr. Jeremy Swan, a world-renowned cardiac specialist and the chief of cardiology at Cedar-Sinai. He was the first—in four long, frustrating years—to unravel the tangle of often misleading clues and conclude that Pann's heart was the main source of her considerable problems. Once he pointed the way, his diagnosis was easily confirmed by others.

Now Pann was waiting for them to open her up and replace a piece of her heart. "Lord God, please let this be the end of it," Pann prayed as she lay quietly on the bed, waiting for her dinner tray.

"Hi, good looking!" Bill walked breathlessly into the room. "Sorry I'm late. A couple unexpected problems came up at work just as I was ready to leave." Bill was a field service manager with Xerox, and while the job allowed him to work his own hours most of the time (not to mention providing one hundred percent insurance coverage of Pann's hospital expenses—no minor detail!), he often put in twelve-to-fourteen-hour days to make up for the time he took off to be with her. "Doctor Matloff been in yet?"

Pann had no sooner said, "No. He should be here soon," than the doctor strode into the room.

Jack Matloff would perform the surgery. He was a big man, with close-cropped silvery hair and a kind but straightforward manner. When she first met him several weeks earlier, Pann's first impression was that he looked better suited to a football field than to an operating room. The idea of his enormous hands doing cardiac surgery on tiny infants was overwhelming. Those hands would soon hold her own life in their grasp.

"How you doing, Pann?" he asked with genuine interest.

"So far, so good." Her smile displayed more confidence than she felt.

"Good. Well, I'm not going to beat around the bush. The surgery we're going to perform on Monday is tricky and unpredictable." He explained how he would replace Pann's mitral valve (the valve on the left side of the heart, between the upper and lower chambers) and possibly, if it looked necessary, the tricuspid valve (on the right side). "To tell you the truth, considering your past history, I don't know that I would have opted to do this surgery if the decision had been left up to me. I'm doing it for two reasons. First, we're in a corner. I see nowhere else to go. You're a young, attractive woman, Pann, with everything to live for and very little chance of surviving another year if things are left the way they are. I *can't* guarantee the results of this operation, but I *can* guarantee what will happen if you do not have it. Second, I'm doing this for Jeremy. Personally, I'm a 'black-and-white' man, myself. I like the odds to be clearly in my favor, and in all honesty, we're working in a gray area here. But Jeremy believes it will work, and he has one of the most uncanny medical sixth senses I've ever known. So we'll give it our all and hope for the best." He patted Pann's hand reassuringly and started toward the door. "We are going to have to run a few tests between now and Monday. Tomorrow I've got you scheduled for an H.I.S. bundle study."

"Oh, no," Pann protested weakly. She had had a similar cardiac catheterization several years before, and the memory of the uncomfortable procedure was still painfully fresh.

"Sorry," he said. "We need to know whether we should implant a pacemaker while we're in there."

The next morning Pann was tense with the unpleasant anticipation of what lay ahead. She knew the test would be done with only a local anesthetic and that she would be conscious the entire time. For Pann, pain had become a relative thing, for rarely was she without it in some form. But even though she had learned how to use relaxation and concentration to "make friends" with the pain, this was one area where practice had not made perfect, and she did not want to face the four-hour ordeal alone.

Since Bill could not be there, Roma Swan, Jeremy's wife and an old friend of Pann's family, offered to take his place. Roma had become a very special person in Pann's life. Roma was diminutive—one of the few people who made Pann feel tall. But she made up for her size by her enormous energy and great warmth. She had originally brought Pann and Jeremy together. During the weeks that followed, the Swans had stepped over the professional boundaries to become personally involved with the Baltzes, even taking K.C. into their home for several days while Pann had some preoperative tests.

Now Roma stood by Pann's side. She wiped Pann's brow with a cool cloth to keep her from fainting and spoke words of encouragement while catheters were inserted through an artery in her groin. Pann could feel the catheters slowly work their way up to her heart. Each catheter was equipped with electrodes, which, when situated in the chambers of her heart, would enable the doctors to tell how well Pann's own internal pacemaker was working. The whole tedious process could be viewed on a monitor, and Pann had a front-row seat. She watched, along with everyone else, as the catheter finally reached its destination. She could also see the catheter as it suddenly passed through the wall that separated the two upper chambers of her heart.

"Did you see that?" someone gasped.

"Is it supposed to do that?" Pann asked in alarm.

"Not exactly," was the vague reply.

Dr. Mandel, who was in charge of the study, ordered his assistants to draw the catheter out of the heart and reinsert it. Once again, it passed through what was obviously a hole in an inside wall of Pann's heart.

Several weeks before, Dr. Matloff had suggested that perhaps Pann had a patent foramen ovale, which is an opening in the heart that all fetuses have, though it generally closes before birth. Occasionally, however, it does not close. For some reason, this opening had not shown up on any of Pann's previous tests. It came as a total surprise. Obviously, this was one way blood clots could be passed to the brain, and it would need to be corrected during the surgery.

As the hours dragged on, Pann found the discomfort increasingly difficult to handle. Besides the catheters inserted near her groin, one had been inserted into a vein in her arm.

Because the veins in Pann's arms had been used so often that they had begun to collapse, the procedure was more difficult than usual. Now her arm ached with increasingly deep pulsations. When she could stand the pain no longer, she asked, "Isn't there something you can give me? An aspirin? Anything?"

The doctor agreed that she could have an aspirin back in her room, and Pann comforted herself with the thought that the end was near. Not just the end of the test, but the end of all the pain, fear, and uncertainty that had overshadowed her life for the past few years. This was Friday. The operation was scheduled for Monday. Just three more days and it would be over. Surely she could make it for just three more days.

Pann lived through Saturday like an astronaut waiting for the final countdown before blast-off. She could feel her nerves winding tighter and tighter with every passing hour.

One by one, her support crew arrived. Bill's brother Steve flew in from Denver. Pann's mother arrived from Seattle. Everyone was geared up for the big day.

Three o'clock on Sunday afternoon, Pann lay there, only half listening to the animated conversations around her. She vainly tried to relax and calm the butterflies in her stomach. Bill was there and her mom and Steve—people she loved, who loved her. Yet somehow, she felt, they were on the other side of a vast chasm. Oh, how she longed to cross over and join them on the side of safety and normalcy. One more day . . .

The door opened and Dr. Mandel entered. After the bundle study, he had run routine clotting tests to see how long it took Pann to stop bleeding. Dr. Mandel was a tender-hearted man. The first time he had read Pann's files, he had been deeply moved, unable to believe that anyone could endure so much pain and bad luck. Now he looked at her with sad, apologetic eyes that warned her that something was wrong.

"Pann, I'm afraid I've got some bad news. We've been

watching you very closely, testing to make sure your blood is clotting as it should. For us to perform surgery, you must stop bleeding in eight minutes or less. The last test we took shows that you are not even close."

"But how can that be?" asked Pann in a stunned voice. "I was fine before. What could have happened?"

"We think it's the aspirin."

"The what?"

"The aspirin. The one we gave you after the bundle study. Apparently it has affected your clotting ability. At least, that's what we think at this point. We'll have to call in a hematologist to be sure. If it is the aspirin, the effects will wear off, and you should be back to normal in a few days. But I'm afraid we'll have to postpone the operation."

Pann sat frozen for a few seconds, paralyzed by the impact of his words. No operation tomorrow. They would have to wait and see. No operation—because of an aspirin. One dumb little aspirin.

"No! I can't take this!" Pann felt the dam of her emotions crack and crumble as tears came in a gush of release. There was no holding back. "You can't do this. I can't take it! You're taking my hope away; can't you see? It's all just been too much . . . too much. It's got to end! We're so close, and now you say we have to wait? What if my condition doesn't change? What if I have another stroke? What if . . . Oh, God, where are You? Where are You?"

Dr. Mandel stood with tears streaming down his face, awkwardly patting Pann's hand. He looked beseechingly at the nurse, then at Bill and Pann's mother. But they too stood weeping. There was nothing to do but let Pann cry. Her racking sobs were like a wail of protest and mourning, not only for today, but for all she had once had and lost and might never have again.

III

DICK AND EILEEN LANGFORD moved their young family from Knoxville, Tennessee, to Highland Park, California, to work with Young Life Ministries in 1954. Southern California seemed the perfect place to raise their family: their son, Richard, then eight years old; and their daughter, Patricia Ann, age four. They put down roots, and when Young Life asked them to move to Colorado, Dick decided instead to accept an offer to serve as director of Christian education at Hollywood Presbyterian Church. Eventually he was ordained by the presbytery.

Patricia Ann, nicknamed "Pann" by her father, was an active and precocious child. Small for her age, she seemed doubly determined to prove she could keep up with her older brother. And for the most part, she did. Other children delighted in teasing her about her name, calling her "Pan American," "pots and pans," and of course, "Peter Pan." While the teasing was tiresome, it taught Pann at an early age the importance of being able to laugh at herself and to value a sense of humor.

There are two kinds of popular girls in high school. The first is the tall, natural beauty, who always looks like she just stepped off the pages of *Seventeen* magazine and is elected homecoming queen as part of her birthright. The other girls are jealous of her, and most of the boys are terrified of her. But she *is* popular. The second kind is the vivacious, energetic girl who makes everyone feel special with her friendly hellos and who usually is elected to the pep squad and student-body leadership. Other girls try to emulate her, and the boys love to date her.

In high school, Pann definitely fit into that second group. Five feet tall, with honey-blond hair and big, expressive blue eyes, Pann had a quick wit and an outgoing personality. She was a natural leader; she was a student-body officer, a cheerleader, and one of the valedictorians of her graduating class. Her parents were proud of her, not only for what she accomplished, but because she did it without compromising her Christian faith. Unlike some "preacher's kids," Pann never went through a rebellious stage or felt it necessary to test the standards by which she had been raised. Instead, she embraced them, finding in them a solid sense of identity upon which to lay the foundation for her life. Later this foundation would prove essential to her survival.

During the summer after her graduation, Pann met Bill Baltz. He too had grown up in the Hollywood Presbyterian Church. He once kidded that his family was so Presbyterian that he was born at the Presbyterian hospital and transferred directly into the church nursery. At first, since he was five years older than Pann, he found little reason to notice Pastor Langford's little girl.

Shortly after his high-school graduation, Bill moved out on

his own and began working to put himself through college at USC. The midsixties—the "Age of Aquarius" and the flower children—were a hard time for a clean-cut, Ivy League type to find an identity. For a while, Bill stopped going to church and attempted to fit in with the "in crowd." But by his senior year in college, he found himself missing the warmth and fellowship he had once enjoyed at church. Through the interest and encouragement of the church's college director, Don Williams, he made his way back to a committed relationship with Jesus Christ.

Not long after Bill had rededicated his life to the Lord, he was talking to a friend after Sunday school when he noticed a small, slender girl in a flowery summer dress and wide-brimmed hat. She was animatedly talking to a group of friends, her conversation punctuated with frequent laughter.

"Who's that?" he asked his friend, pointing in her direction.

"That's Pann Langford. You remember her, don't you?"

Bill remember her all right, when she was a scrawny little ten-year-old with buckteeth and braces. *The miracle of the butterfly,* he thought in amazement.

Over the next few weeks Bill and Pann got to know each other. He was impressed by the thoughtful insights Pann shared with him. She was stimulating and intelligent, and he enjoyed talking with her. It was easy to open up and be himself.

As for Pann, she was immediately attracted to the tall, athletic young man with the serious, though often amusing manner. She found herself thinking about him more and more, and wondering why other guys found her to be prime dating material, but not Bill. He *seemed* to like her. He sought her out after church for long talks. But when he went out on a date, it was usually with some tall, stunning beauty on his arm—rarely the same girl twice.

One Sunday evening after church, Pann and Bill were deep in conversation. Her brother, Richard, interrupted to say he was leaving.

"That's all right. I'll take Pann home," Bill answered.

Pann felt her heart leap at Bill's unexpected offer. But her joy was short-lived as she heard Richard reply, "Sorry. Mom wants her home early. She needs to get under the vaporizer."

Lord, if You're coming again soon, now would be a good time, Pann silently groaned, her cheeks burning with humiliation. She had recently recovered from one of her frequent bouts with pneumonia, an ailment that had plagued her childhood and put her in bed for over a month that summer. Her family was understandably concerned. But on the way home, Pann gave her brother a heated lecture on the dangers of tactless concern.

Shortly after the vaporizer episode, Bill finally asked Pann for a date, and their relationship rapidly grew to a heartfelt commitment. When fall came, Pann started college at the University of Redlands, but the beautiful campus was wasted on her. She talked to Bill daily on the phone and lived for the weekends when she could see him. By this time, Bill had a full-time job with Signal Oil and Gas and was attending night school at USC. Their schedules were busy and the distance was a difficulty. Still, they managed to spend almost every spare minute together.

Pann kept a big bulletin board over her desk for mementos of their times together. She called this giant collage of pictures, cards, ticket stubs, and letters her "Bill board." Not one to be outdone, Bill kept a picture of Pann by his bed and affectionately referred to it as his "bed Pann."

The next year, Pann transferred to UCLA so she and Bill could be closer. Her parents liked Bill and were reassured by the fact that he would be close by, since Pann's father had accepted an associate pastorship at the University Church in Seattle, Washington.

It was a clear, sunny November afternoon. Bill and Pann sat quietly, enjoying the deepening blue of the sky and the pine-scented nip in the air as they drove the winding mountain road leading to Forest Home Campgrounds above San Bernardino. It was Bill's birthday, and they were celebrating it with a day away. Pann absently fingered the camera in her lap. Bill had borrowed it from a friend, to see if he wanted to buy a similar one, and Pann had agreed to play guinea pig for the camera.

After taking a number of scenic shots around Lake Mears, Pann and Bill made their way to the little prayer chapel. "Pann, I want to get a picture of us here together," Bill said, looking around for the best place to prop the camera. "You stand by the altar and let me focus on you. Then I'll set the automatic timer and run up beside you."

"Okay," said Pann. "This is great! Sure hope it works."

"Me too," said Bill earnestly, fussing with the camera to make sure everything was set just right. Finally he seemed satisfied. "All right, I'm going to set the timer. You ready?"

"All set."

"Okay, here goes." Bill set the device and rushed to the front. But instead of standing at Pann's side, as she expected, he fell to one knee, grabbed her hand, and said, "Pann, I love you. Will you marry me?"

"Yes!" Pann squealed in delight as the camera clicked, capturing the moment forever.

Back in the car, Bill had Pann open the glove compartment, where she found a small box containing a diamond engagement ring. "Oh, it's beautiful! And it fits perfectly," Pann said as Bill slipped it on her finger. "You must have been planning this for a long time."

Bill, in fact, had been making plans for months. He had even talked to Pann's father before the Langfords left for Washington. When Pann and Bill called to tell them the good news, Dick Langford replied, "Well, you had me worried, Bill. It's been so long since we talked, I was afraid you'd changed your mind!"

Ten months later, in September of 1969, Bill and Pann were married. Their first year of marriage was a busy one. Bill had changed jobs and was working full time as a salesman for the Xerox Corporation while finishing night school at USC. Pann continued to work toward her teaching degree at UCLA and worked part-time. They were also involved with the Hollywood Presbyterian Young Marrieds and became a part of a small share-prayer-care group formed by a number of close friends. Couples from this group would provide a core of spiritual and practical support that Bill and Pann would find invaluable in the difficult years ahead.

In 1971 Bill and Pann graduated from their respective schools, and Pann went on to complete a year of student teaching. By the fall of 1972, she was ready to take on her own class. Since Bill was working in El Monte and Pann had been hired by the Arcadia School District, they split the distance and found a lovely Spanish-style house in San Gabriel.

Pann loved teaching, and her enthusiasm infected her young students with the joy of learning. Finally the long years of preparation were over. She was doing what she wanted to do. The only shadow cast on that first year of teaching was a bad case of pneumonia that kept her away from her class for a number of weeks. Pann's second year of teaching was also marred by illness. She was hospitalized for three weeks with what was diagnosed as a lung infection and inflammation of the heart muscle. Both Bill and Pann were frightened to hear the doctors talk about a possible heart problem. How could someone so young—Pann was then twenty-four—have a heart problem?

The results of an electrocardiogram were not completely normal, but the doctors seemed more concerned about the results of a bone scan that showed a suspicious-looking area around Pann's sternum (the bone that runs between the breasts). A bone-marrow test was scheduled.

Pann had never experienced extreme pain. Toothaches, bellyaches, headaches, a skinned knee, a sliced finger—these were her frame of reference. None of them prepared her for the intensity of the pain she felt as the long needle was inserted and the bone marrow removed. Afterward she lay thinking about all the little children with leukemia or other catastrophic diseases who are forced to go through that torture repeatedly. *How do they survive it?* she thought in agony. *I know I couldn't.*

But the pain faded; and more importantly, so did Pann and Bill's fear of cancer. The test result was negative, and in the rush of their relief, the abnormal electrocardiogram was all but forgotten.

Bill and Pann began to talk about starting a family. Children were important to them, and they had it all planned: first a boy, then a girl, then maybe one or two more for good measure.

In light of the radioactive testing she'd been through, the doctors warned Pann to wait six months before getting pregnant. But as soon as Bill and Pann got the all clear, they put their plan into action. In fact, Pann conceived so quickly, Bill often teased her that she walked out of the doctor's office and was pregnant by the time she walked in the front door at home!

Pregnancy was a wonderful experience for Pann. She had heard that it often clears up minor health problems, and in Pann's case, that appeared to be true. Her body exulted in its condition, becoming full and rounded in a most attractive way. Her eyes gleamed and her cheeks were rosy. She felt better than she had in years, experiencing few of the discomforts of early pregnancy.

Only her occasional fainting spells were the least bit

suspicious. But since she was slightly anemic, a condition common during pregnancy, the doctors attributed her blackouts to that. While Pann was not concerned about her fainting spells, they were a bit of an inconvenience, coming on her at any time and with little warning.

It was September 1974, Pann's seventh month of pregnancy. She and Bill had gone to a church party the night before. They had come home late and dropped exhausted into bed. The next morning Pann was up early, puttering quietly around the house to let Bill catch a few extra winks. She picked up a wastepaper basket and was on the way out the back door to the trash can when her head began to pound and darkness dropped on her like a ten-pound weight. Finding nothing to hold on to, she fell down the back steps and landed hard on her foot. She heard the crack and knew something was broken before the first waves of nauseating pain even hit.

Pann's cries woke Bill. In a panic, he jumped out of bed and ran to her aid. He rushed her to the emergency room at the hospital, where the foot was set and put in a cast.

The next few weeks taught Pann a fact of life: Most people show little sympathy for a pregnant woman on crutches. They're too busy laughing! Even fellow "expectees" in Pann and Bill's natural-childbirth class couldn't suppress their smiles. It is always a challenge to get a pregnant woman down on the floor and back up again, but add a broken foot in a cast, and it's darn near impossible! When she walked into her Red Cross class in baby care, the instructor took one look and hooted, "Honey, how are they ever going to get you into the stirrups?"

Fortunately the cast was removed several weeks before the baby came. Early on the morning of November 26, Pann's water broke and her contractions began. At first they were so mild, Pann was convinced there was no need for immediate action. But after they had come every five minutes for half an hour, Bill could stand it no longer. "Don't you think we should call the doctor?" he asked, nervously throwing back the bed covers.

"No. I think we ought to get some more sleep," Pann answered, nestling farther down in the warm bed.

"Well, *I* think we ought to call the doctor!" Bill replied.

Pann listened as he dialed the doctor's number and announced with authority, "Hello, this is Bill Baltz. I think my wife is getting pregnant!"

Pann discreetly buried her head in the pillow and laughed through her next contraction.

Later that morning, K.C. was born.

IV

"Hush little baby, don't say a word;
Mama's gonna buy you a mocking bird . . ."

PANN SANG the lullaby entreatingly as she rocked her baby to quiet his cries. Kenneth Chandler Baltz, called K.C., was almost three months old and was going through a colicky period that was as hard on his tired young mother as it was on him.

Pann and Bill's delight in their firstborn increased daily, just as their energy decreased with each successive sleepless night. To add to Pann's physical exhaustion, the foot she had broken had not healed well. A calcium deposit had formed, making it almost impossible for her to put on her shoe. The previous Thursday she'd had the bone spur removed. The procedure had been done under a general anesthetic and had required an overnight stay in the hospital. Now, as she felt the warm little body in her arms relax into sleep, she became aware of an unreal buzzing sensation in her head.

"Honey, come get the baby and put him to bed, will you?" Pann called, grateful that it was Saturday and Bill was home. "I'm going to lie down for a while."

Pann made her way unsteadily to the bedroom. Stretching out on the bed, she was aware of the ache in her foot and a slight nausea that convinced her she was totally exhausted. Two or three hours of unbroken sleep would make a world of difference. But her sleep was restless, and when she awoke, she felt worse than when she had lain down. Her head felt like someone had blown it up with a tire pump. It was hard for her to catch her breath. Waves of panic and disorientation washed over her as she lay there, trying to gain enough control to get off the bed. Finally, after a couple of unsuccessful attempts, she was able to get up and walk with shaky steps into the living room, where Bill sat reading.

"I feel really sick. Something's wrong."

Bill looked up to see is wife collapse like a rag doll on the floor. Then her body stiffened and her back arched in a generalized convulsion.

The next couple of hours were a blur. The paramedics brought an ambulance to the door. Lights flashed. Sirens screamed. In a daze, Bill watched as his wife, gasping for breath and groaning, was carried out the door on a stretcher.

Bill called Gloria Kilian, Pann's friend and prayer partner, to see if she would watch K.C. Gloria dropped everything to respond to Bill's call for help.

By the time Bill arrived at the hospital, things were well in hand. Pann had been given a shot to help calm her breathing, and a doctor was examining her. Although her pulse was fast and her color was bad, the doctor felt there was nothing to be alarmed about. In light of Pann's recent foot operation, it was his opinion that the spell was probably a delayed reaction to the anesthetic, or possibly a simple attack of hysteria had caused Pann to hyperventilate. Either way, he felt she would be all right in a day or two, and after giving her another shot to knock her out for the next twelve hours, he allowed Bill to take her home.

Pann spent the next day in bed, feeling as if a mule had kicked her. Her head still felt like an inflated balloon, and her body ached with a variety of unnatural sensations. Frequently when Bill checked on her, he found her unresponsive, and a couple of times she passed out completely, her head jerking in convulsions.

Jerry Calloway, a friend of Bill's who was going through his medical residency, stopped by that afternoon. He took one look at Pann and insisted she have a thorough checkup. The problem was deciding who should do it. Pann had an obstetrician because she'd just had a baby, a foot specialist because of her surgery, and a respiratory specialist because of her respiratory infection the year before. But like most people, Pann and Bill had never established a relationship with a good family doctor who could keep track of all the pieces and put together a clear, overall picture of Pann's situation. A family doctor would have been able to recommend the right specialist for any particular problem and would have kept an organized file of the different findings, to make sure nothing was overlooked or misplaced.

As it was, Pann asked her obstetrician for a recommendation when she called to make an appointment for K.C., who, in the spirit of things, had developed a terrible cough. The obstetrician recommended that Pann see a neurologist. Both appointments were scheduled for the next day.

First thing on Monday morning, February 24, 1975, Bill's mother arrived to drive Pann and K.C. to their respective appointments. The morning went by in a haze for Pann, who was sufficiently out of it to require a wheelchair to get to and from the car. The seriousness of the situation still hadn't hit home; surely this was just a case of some new, superpowerful flu bug or perhaps an inner-ear infection.

After being reassured that K.C.'s problem was simply an old-fashioned cold, Pann and her mother-in-law went to the neurologist's office. It didn't take the doctor long to discern that there was something seriously wrong. The standard neurological checkup showed that Pann's reflexes were weak on the right side of her body and her right eye was beginning to droop. Pann could tell from his expression that he didn't like what he saw, but she was surprised when he insisted that she check into the hospital—immediately.

"Go home, pack a bag, and come right back," he said sternly, leaving no room for discussion.

As they left the waiting room, Pann overheard the nurse talking to the admissions desk at the hospital. The words "seizure precaution" and "neuro floor" sent a cold chill down her spine. Countless questions flooded her mind. What's wrong with me? Who's going to take care of K.C.? How will Bill get along? Where is God in the midst of this?

The first thing Pann did at home was to call Bill. With stunned calmness, they discussed what needed to be done. Their greatest concern was for K.C., and Pann's most comforting thought was to ask her mother to fly down from Seattle. All it took was a phone call and Mrs. Langford was set to arrive the next day. Bill's mother offered to stay until then. Next, Pann called her cousin Phyllis for a ride to the hospital. Bill would meet them there. Again the answer was an unhesitating yes.

At the hospital Pann was admitted to the neurological ward on the second floor. She learned later that the second floor was reserved for those needing critical care. Her eyes widened at the sight of the bed in her room; the four rails were padded with blankets.

Seeing the look on her face, the nurse explained, "That's simply a seizure precaution. If you have another seizure, you won't hurt yourself. Don't let it worry you."

"Oh," Pann replied, hardly comforted by the thought that other seizures were possible.

After helping Pann into her hospital gown and settling her into bed, Bill gave her a big hug and kiss good-bye, teasing that she looked like a mouse in a shoe box in the big enclosed bed. "Mouse" was his pet name for Pann, a name he had started using while they were dating, claiming she squeaked like a mouse when she got excited and was always munching on cheese and nuts.

Pann laughed gamely at Bill's attempt to reassure her and squeezed his hand to let him know she was all right. But the easy words and laughter were a thin disguise for the fear that filled both their hearts.

During the next few days, Pann was subjected to a seemingly endless series of tests: brain scans, blood tests, electroencephalograms, EMI scans, and X rays, none of which pinpointed the cause of the problem. At the same time, Pann's right side continued to weaken. By Friday the doctors decided that an angiogram was necessary, although it was a risky procedure, requiring that dye be injected into the brain. Blindness or a stroke were only two of the possible dangers, but at this point, the doctors suspected Pann might have a brain tumor, and the angiogram would either confirm or deny their suspicion. The only other possibility was that Pann was already in the midst of a stroke.

Pann felt a nervous giggle threaten to escape as she listened to the serious-faced young doctor explain the situation. The idea of a brain tumor was terrifying, but a stroke? Where did they dig these doctors up? Nobody has a stroke at twenty-five!

The angiogram was scheduled for the next morning. Immediately Bill and Mrs. Langford began calling friends in Seattle and Los Angeles to ask them to pray about the test. God answered those prayers—but not exactly as they expected.

During the night, Pann's condition worsened significantly. Her blood pressure dropped and her symptoms intensified. By morning there was no longer any question. Pann was definitely having a stroke. Had the doctors attempted an angiogram, she would have died.

Stroke! The word echoed through Pann's thoughts as she desperately tried to make some sense of what was happening. Everyone lives with the knowledge that tragic things can happen. You can step off a curb and be hit by a bus or wake up one morning to find a lump in your breast. These things are shocking, and we're never prepared for them. Somehow, though, they are an accepted part of the uncertain world in which we live.

But strokes are for older people, not for vibrant young women with small babies to care for, she thought. *It must be a mistake . . . some malicious practical joke.*

Yet Pann could not deny the obvious as she watched her body become weaker and more distorted. By Saturday afternoon the muscles on the right side of her face had completely collapsed, giving her the surrealistic appearance of a painting by Dali. Her right arm and leg were virtually paralyzed.

Still, the full impact of what was happening didn't hit home until Pann's mother came to see her.

Eileen Langford: "I had asked for a week's leave of absence from my teaching job in Seattle to take care of K.C. I knew Pann was sick, but nothing could have prepared me for the sight of my daughter in that hospital bed. I'd seen stroke victims before, but they were elderly, and although I felt outrage at the indignity of once strong and healthy people being made helpless and dependent, their age made it seem like part of the natural cycle of life.

"When I walked into the hospital room and saw the misshapen little lump of humanity in the bed, I no more thought it was Pann than the man in the moon. I would have turned and walked out again, if I hadn't felt Bill give me a gentle nudge. Suddenly I realized: that's my girl. I rushed to gather her in my arms, holding her close to my chest until I was able to control my shock. We talked, and somehow I held back my tears until the visit was over. Bill and I made it back to the car, then he held me while I cried.

"In the years that followed, I saw Pann in even worse condition, but nothing ever hit me as hard as that first time."

After the stroke was diagnosed, Pann was placed on heparin, a blood thinner designed to dissolve offending blood clots. In a few days it was obvious the medication was doing its job; Pann was on an upward swing.

At this point, one of the doctors sat down with her and drew a picture to help her understand what had happened. He explained how a small blood clot can form (why it formed, he did not know) and how, as blood flows past it, other little platelets cling to it, causing it to grow. Eventually it grows large enough to block off a blood vessel altogether, which in turn cuts off oxygen to the brain cells that vessel feeds. Without oxygen the cells die, causing the stroke; once brain cells are dead, they do not regenerate.

Fortunately, we use only a small portion of our brain cells and others can be trained to take the place of those that have been damaged. This is where the tedious and often painful process of rehabilitation comes in.

A rehabilitation ward is a world unto itself, a sort of halfway point between the worlds of the sick and the well. It is here that the extent of a patient's recovery—and therefore the quality of life thereafter—is determined. Those who have the greatest success are those who have the determination to recover the use of muscles that have forgotten their basic functions.

At first Pann found it all overwhelming, and she fought severe attacks of depression and self-pity. She hit a real low point the day a form arrived from the school district that required her signature. She wept as her mother pressed a pen between Pann's fingers and lifted her lifeless hand to guide it along the dotted line.

But before long Pann's feisty spirit began to revive, refusing to be dominated by doubt and despair. Bill knew she was on her way to recovery the evening he and his parents joined her in the hospital dining room for dinner. After the meal Pann pushed herself back from the table and announced she was going to *walk* back to her room. Bill's first reaction was to object, but one look at his wife's determined face convinced him he should let her try. He knew the embarrassment she felt at having to use a wheelchair. So with a resigned smile, he offered his arm as, step by step, she dragged her right foot down the long corridors to her room. It took half an hour, but they made it.

After that, Pann threw herself into therapy with zeal. The doctors, after all, had expressed confidence that at her age she could make a complete recovery. If she stayed off the birth-control pills, which they felt had caused the blood clot and her stroke, she could go on to lead a perfectly normal life, without any fear of future problems.

A typical day of rehabilitation began at 6:30 A.M. The nurse would enter the room with a cheerful "good morning" and a glass of warm prune juice. The patients in the rehab unit joked about the "royal flush" after breakfast. Pann joined in the laughter but discreetly poured the juice into the potted plants beside her bed. The plants flourished, and so did she.

After breakfast the morning was divided into two sessions. The first, physical therapy, concentrated on working the large muscles in Pann's right arm and leg to help her develop a better walking pattern. Next came occupational therapy, which dealt with the more refined movements needed to accomplish basic daily activities such as lifting a fork to her mouth and brushing her teeth. The sessions were repeated in the afternoon, which left Pann thoroughly exhausted by the end of the day.

Pann's stay in the hospital was almost as exhausting for

Bill. Continuing to carry a full work load at Xerox, he would leave the office, check in on K.C., then head straight to the hospital to spend the evening with Pann. Bill's visits were a lifeline for Pann; they reassured her that she was loved and reminded her of all the good things she had to go home to.

There is no question that the hardest part of her hospitalization was her separation from K.C. Later she described her feelings in her journal: "Sometimes it seemed as if my heart had a heavy ache in it from wanting to hold him so badly. Getting to see him at the end of my first week, even though I had to be on a stretcher, made all the nightmare qualities of the week and the loss of my right side worth bearing."

After the first week, Eileen Langford returned to her job in Seattle, which left Bill in a quandary over what to do with K.C. Soon, however, the love and selfless giving of their friends began to show itself. After Mrs. Langford's departure, Melody, K.C.'s godmother and one of Pann's long-time friends, volunteered to come to the house. She brought her six-month-old child with her. Then Gloria and Paul Kilian took care of K.C., keeping him until Pann was released. This was the first of many times the Kilians would open their home to the child, who was to become an integral part of their family over the next few years.

Gloria Kilian: "It just seemed natural that we should take over with K.C. Our own baby was eighteen months old; and our schedule had just gotten back to normal. Still, it didn't seem like a particular burden to start 2:00 A.M. feedings all over again. K.C. was a darling baby, a joy to take care of.

"We got to have K.C. during all those important, wonderful weeks when a baby is discovering the world and his own body. I remember going to the hospital after Pann's stroke and explaining that K.C. had just focused on his finger for the first time. I was so excited, but she seemed detached because of her condition and medication. Later she looked back and realized what she missed."

Pann found it very hard to accept the loss of so many precious "firsts." She wanted to be the first to see her son smile or roll over, and the thought of all she was missing would plunge her into depression and cause her to cry out to God the age-old question: Why me? But inevitably, at her lowest moments, Pann would look up and see Bill coming through the door, often with K.C. snuggled in his arms. The sight of them would help lift the dark clouds and remind her that self-pity was a waste of time. She couldn't afford it—not if she was going to get well, go home, and get on with the life God had given her.

Five weeks after she had entered, Pann left the hospital. She had ninety percent of the use of her right arm, and although her right foot still dragged, she was able to walk with a cane. One of the first things she did at home was write a letter thanking people for their prayers and support.

> The Lord has been very good. I am now at home after a month. At the start of that month, I was almost completely paralyzed on my right side, unable to write my name. My face is now completely normal, I am walking, and I am writing this letter slowly but surely with my right hand.
>
> We ask your continued support in prayer for the months of therapy and hard work that lie ahead on the road to recovery. I count myself very blessed with such super friends, family, my mother, who were here to help us out, and the most loving and supportive husband in the world.
>
> Much love,
> Pann

V

PANN'S FIRST WEEKS at home were an odd mixture of highs and lows. Although she was happy to be with Bill and K.C., she couldn't forget the violent assault her body had experienced. Her arm and hand continued to improve, but her right leg and foot stubbornly resisted the therapy that she received three times a week. While her faith remained strong, her emotions had suffered a traumatic blow, the full effects of which she had only begun to feel.

Like many Christians, Pann and Bill had mistakenly believed that their relationship with God somehow insured them against major catastrophe. Before that day in February, their lives seemed to prove that theory. But the stroke abruptly brought Pann and Bill face-to-face with the reality that our commitment to Christ—and His commitment to us—are no guarantees of safe passage through this life. This realization left Pann feeling strangely betrayed and frightened. Anger and resentment began to surface, feelings that were not easy for Pann to deal with. Since Pann had been raised to believe that anger was not an acceptable Christian response, guilt and self-denial were added to her boiling kettle of emotions.

Finding it difficult to verbalize her feelings, Pann began to write in her journal the things she dared not voice. Her first day back at church produced a particularly strong and unexpected emotional response.

> We went to church today. It was hard. The chaplain from Hollywood Presbyterian Hospital spoke. Hearing him made some of my own feelings surface. For instance, I realized that I've had so many health problems, I'm afraid I might die, and I need to settle with Bill what the plan would be for K.C. if anything should happen to me.
>
> But the hardest thing for me was so many caring, well-meaning friends saying how good I looked and how well I was walking, when I wanted to scream, "I'm not walking well, and I don't know if I ever will! I'm so slow. I hate having to think about every step I take!" I feel so discouraged with the walk. It is hard for me to feel that I'll ever walk right again, much less run or skip.
>
> It seems as if nobody wants to listen to how I feel about what happened to me. They just want to pat me on the back and breathe a sigh of relief that they don't have to worry anymore. Then I have guilty feelings for feeling this way about people who are being so nice to me and for being depressed when I *am* lucky. It could have been so much worse.

For Bill, the readjustment was easier. Of course Pann's stroke had been a jolt that had left him shaken and wondering how God could let this happen. And if it had to happen to someone, why not him instead of Pann? But once the worst was over and Pann was on the mend, Bill was eager to get on with their lives. He saw Pann's recovery as nothing more than a temporary inconvenience. Certainly his feelings toward her hadn't changed. To him she was still the most beautiful, desirable woman in the world—limp and all.

These were words Pann needed to hear, since one of her most desperate battles was against the feeling that somehow she was less appealing because of her ordeal. How could Bill love her the way she was? And what about K.C.? She certainly was not living up to the high standard of motherhood she had set for herself. She couldn't even take care of her own baby without help.

By May, Pann's right foot was still not responding to therapy. In fact, it seemed to drag even more, causing her no end of embarrassment as she stumbled over doorsills and any slightly uneven ground.

One day she was sitting alone in the living room. K.C. was asleep and the house was oppressively quiet. Pann felt the old self-pity and depression begin to mount, and she felt helpless to stop it. Her misery swelled to the point of becoming physical pain, and her eyes overflowed with hot, bitter tears. "Oh, God, how could You let this happen?" she cried out. "What have I done? How have I failed?" Her words tumbled over one another in a rush, expressing all her fear and frustration. Eventually the torrent of words slowed to a trickle and then died into silence as Pann sat empty and exhausted. Then the Lord began to speak to Pann's heart, gently but firmly expressing His love for her, recounting His faithfulness over the past months, and reaffirming His commitment to her future. But there were certain requirements that Pann needed to acknowledge. It wasn't going to be easy. Just as she needed to discipline her body to have it healed and restored, so too she needed to discipline her mind and emotions.

The next day Pann sat down with a new notebook. Staring for a moment at the unblemished whiteness of the first page, she picked three markers from the rainbow of colors at her side. At the top of the page she wrote, in letters two inches high, "Yes, Lord."

Pann hummed as she carefully colored the letters blue, pink, and purple. Then, in thoughtful silence, she listed the things she had heard God speak to her the day before.

1. I shall know that God loves me just as I am.
2. I shall know that God can use me just as I am.
3. I shall know that God has a plan for me just as I am.
4. I shall not get in God's way by feeling sorry for myself.
5. I shall not speak of my disability unless I am asked.
6. I shall remember that there are others much worse than I am.
7. I shall not apologize for things I cannot do because of my disability.
8. I shall use what I have been through to help others whenever I can.
9. I shall remember that I have given God all the hurt, anger, and bitterness, and that He has indeed taken it.

Pann was determined to do her best to live up to these simple guidelines, and things took a turn for the better. Shortly afterward, her therapist decided Pann should try wearing a brace on her leg. While she wasn't crazy about the idea, she found the brace made walking considerably easier and was barely noticeable under her pants.

Her relationship with Bill also improved. After her first few weeks at home, Bill had become less and less available as a sounding board. It wasn't that he had stopped being concerned; he simply had pressures of his own that had been put on the back burner for a long time, and he was losing patience with his role as the constant giver. He needed some emotional "shoring up" himself, and Pann realized she needed to be there for him if he was going to continue to be a source of strength for her.

Focusing on someone else's problems was therapeutic for Pann. While she and Bill still had unavoidable moments of stress and disagreement, Pann's notebook testified to the healthy way in which they handled them. After a particularly vehement disagreement, Pann recorded the outcome in her journal by pasting a florist's card at the bottom of the page; it read, "I'm sorry. May we grow together?" Bill signed it, "Blatz." The card came with a single red rose and inspired Pann to write, "How special to love each other in Christ and to both reflect on our faults in a disagreement!"

The next few pages in Pann's notebook reflected the joy and optimism of the following weeks. One big daisy declared, "Things That Made Today Special," such as "The new brace, which almost lets me walk normally," and, "My first trip alone to the grocery store."

Another page began, "Blessings of My Week," and showed an ear of corn and a cluster of grapes. On the corn were written such things as "good talks with Bill," "super letters," and "answers to prayer in prayer partners." On the grapes were clustered "walks so well," "K.C.'s new schedule," "good reading," "flowers in the garden," and "Freedom!" At the bottom of the page, Pann wrote Psalm 4:6–8 (NEB) as a declaration of her heart:

> There are many who say, "If only we might be prosperous again! But the light of thy presence has fled from us, O Lord." Yet in my heart thou hast put more happiness than they enjoyed when there was corn and wine in plenty. Now I will lie down in peace, and sleep; for thou alone, O Lord, makest me live unafraid.

The end of May found Bill and Pann beginning to put the whole bad experience behind them and acknowledging that good things had come from it. The only symptom that persisted was a funny feeling in Pann's chest. If Pann had had a family doctor, who could oversee her total condition, things might have gone differently. But as it was, the neurologist had cleared Pann after three months, and she was no longer under a doctor's care.

Again God used Jerry Calloway. During one visit, he asked, as everyone did, how Pann was doing.

"Fine," she answered automatically.

"Good," he said. "Now tell me how you're *really* doing."

"Well," she replied, "I *do* have these funny feelings in my chest."

He asked her to describe them, and then advised, "You really should see an internist and have that checked out."

Bill and Pann asked around and were given the name of Dr. Ralph Martin. When Pann called to make an appointment, she was told she would have to wait several weeks unless there was a cancellation. Two days later a cancellation came through and she found herself hooked up to an electrocardiogram in Dr. Martin's office.

It seems amazing that, with all the tests Pann had been put through at the hospital, Dr. Martin was the first to seriously check her heart. After listening to her heartbeat for a while, he said, "You don't have a normal EKG. Has anyone ever told you that you have a heart murmur?"

"No," Pann replied in total surprise.

"Well, I think you should see a cardiologist. It's just possible that your heart had something to do with your stroke."

Pann left the office in a minor state of shock. First the stroke and now a heart murmur? Why hadn't anyone heard it before? Years later the doctors would theorize that Pann's heart murmur was very small before her pregnancy and simply escaped detection. During her pregnancy, her heart had swollen in size to accommodate the baby. Then the troubled valve, which was usually too large for its opening, fit correctly for the first time, eliminating any murmur during her pregnancy. That would also account for Pann's good health during her pregnancy.

But after K.C.'s birth, the heart abruptly shrank back to normal size, worsening the condition and leaving Pann with the obvious murmur the doctor now heard.

Dr. Martin arranged for Pann to see the head of cardiology at a local hospital. The cardiologist confirmed that Pann did have a murmur caused by a prolapsed mitral valve. This is not an uncommon condition; about ten percent of all women have a valve prolapse to some degree, and in ninety-five percent of those cases, the condition is benign.

The doctor put Pann on a heart monitor for twenty-four hours to determine if medication was needed. He also did an echocardiogram to evaluate how big the prolapse was. The test showed that Pann's was significant and also that she was in an abnormal atrial rhythm. The cardiologist suggested that she be put on a medication called Inderal. Dr. Martin, however, vetoed the idea. He felt Pann's condition was not serious enough to warrant putting her on a drug that she might have to take for the rest of her life.

Pann found the idea of a heart condition extremely frightening, but this time she was determined not to allow her fears to pull her down. Instead, strengthened by a new awareness of God's power in her life, she faced them head-on. On June 23 she wrote in her notebook:

Reflections of My Heart

What I Know—A valve in my heart does not work correctly. This condition should be benign. The outside chance is that it could cause sudden death in rare cases.

What I'm Afraid Of—(1) That I will die. (2) That I will have to leave Bill and K.C. (3) That I can never be pregnant again. (4) That I will have to live with pain and discomfort. (5) That my mother can't take this one more problem.

What I Must Cope With—Pain and the possibility of death.

Conclusions—(1) I cannot cope on my own; therefore God must cope for me. He must be ever present in my thoughts. (2) Time will be a great healer in the hurt and fear I feel. (3) I have to feel that in all this, God has a very special purpose for my life, for Bill and me as a couple in ministry to others. (4) I can be grateful for the early privilege of facing life and death squarely and living each day to the fullest.

VI

IT WAS THE FIRST SUNDAY in July. The air was warm and blessedly smog free. Pann moved around her kitchen, fixing breakfast with a renewed feeling of confidence and well-being. More than four months had passed since her stroke, and almost everything was back to normal. Only the brace on her leg testified to her past troubles. On a day like today, it was easy for Pann to believe that even that would be gone soon.

K.C. sat in his highchair, noisily beating a spoon on the metal tray and shrieking in delight. Pann called Bill to the table and sat down to feed her budding young musician a bowl of warm cereal.

"Come on, K.C. Let's put that spoon to good use." Pann snatched the spoon, filled it, and popped it into K.C.'s mouth just as he opened it to complain. But tasting the sweet gruel sliding across his tongue, he smiled a toothless grin of approval, allowing half the cereal to run down his chin.

Bill and Pann laughed. It was an amazing expression of God's love and faithfulness that, despite the tumultuous months since his birth, K.C. was happy and well-adjusted, having been surrounded by people who took extra care to hold him and love him and reassure him.

As she spooned the cereal into K.C.'s ever-ready mouth, Pann oohed and aahed over every swallow. Suddenly the right side of her son's face faded into darkness. It looked as if she were watching television and a portion of the screen went black. She blinked to clear her vision, looked at Bill, and shook her head in jerky little motions.

"Pann, what is it?" Bill asked, tempted to laugh at his wife's strange behavior. At first he thought she was trying to make K.C. laugh, but her look of panic as she bolted to the bathroom alarmed him. In the bathroom he found Pann staring hard at her reflection in the mirror.

"I can't see part of my face! It's like a giant jigsaw puzzle, and these pieces are missing." Pann's voice broke with emotion. She urgently rubbed her right cheek and watched in horror as her hand disappeared in and out of the area of darkness. "Bill, what's happening? I can't see part of my face. Help me!"

Bill took his sobbing wife into his arms and reassured her that everything would be all right. Silently he prayed that his words were true. He was as frightened as she was.

Helping Pann to the bed, Bill continued to hold her while trying to make sense of what was happening. Maybe it was emotional and would go away if she could just relax. After all, she had been doing a lot lately. Maybe she had overdone it and was just exhausted.

Eventually, the black hole disappeared and left a faint sparkling effect in its place. But Pann was shaken. First thing on Monday, she called Dr. Martin, who seemed as perplexed as she was. That he didn't appear alarmed was a comfort. He simply said to let him know if it happened again.

By Wednesday, Pann was feeling well enough to keep a dinner engagement with an old friend she was eager to see. Sondra had been one of Pann's best friends in high school; so when she called to invite Bill and Pann to her parents' home for dinner, they had happily accepted.

It was good to see Sondra again. Although their lives had gone in separate directions after graduation, being together brought back old feelings of closeness. Their conversation was full of laughter and good-natured groans about the "good old days."

Sondra's parents had a lovely home. The dining room was warm with candlelight and good cheer as they sat down to dinner. But before long, Pann became aware of a funny feeling in her head. The candles began to flicker in a crazy, distorted way, and the room started to spin. Suddenly she wasn't sure what to do with the fork in her hand; she let it drop into her lap. Fortunately, only Bill seemed aware of the trouble she was having.

"Pann—you all right?" he asked softly.

"I think I need to lie down," she answered in a voice that echoed distantly in her ears.

Excusing themselves, they went into one of the bedrooms, where Bill took Pann's pulse. It was fast.

"I think I'd better call Dr. Martin." He grabbed the phone on the night stand. Dr. Martin could not be reached, but the doctor on call told him to bring Pann right to the hospital.

All of this happened in only ten or fifteen minutes, but by the time they left the house, Pann could no longer walk, and her speech was beginning to be affected. Sondra and her parents watched in stunned silence as Bill, who was unwilling to wait for an ambulance, carried Pann to the car.

On the way to the hospital, Bill felt as if he were in a bizarre dream. *None of this was real. It couldn't be.* "Oh, God, please. Help us. Don't let it happen again. Please, God. Please." Bill mumbled the prayer over and over, glancing nervously at the limp, unconscious woman next to him. Once or twice he thought she might be dead. Then he would see Pann's chest heave, and his knees would shake with relief.

He struggled to keep his foot from pushing the gas pedal to the floor. "Don't speed. Don't be reckless. Just get her to the hospital," he kept admonishing himself. The drive seemed to take forever. Finally they pulled into the emergency entrance of the hospital, where white-coated staff were waiting.

The doctor's examination showed a marked weakness down the right side of Pann's body. As she drifted in and out of consciousness, she heard one person say, "Another stroke," and something about a spinal tap. When she opened her mouth to protest, only a confused garble of words escaped her lips. She knew what she wanted to say, but somehow the words got short-circuited between her brain and her mouth. She lay groaning, unable to express her fear and disbelief. *How could this be happening?* An hour ago she was sitting at dinner, talking and laughing with an old friend, and now she was lying on a hard, cold table, unable to speak and surrounded by grave-faced doctors preparing to do a spinal tap.

Crazy thoughts went through her head as she felt them hook her up to an IV. She envisioned Rod Serling walking through the door with a microphone in his hand, announcing in his familiar hushed voice, "We see here Pann Baltz, who has just started a journey through that strange and distant world called the Twilight Zone!" Music . . . "Da Da Dee Da Da Dee Dum!"

After the spinal tap, Pann was told to lie flat on her back to help control the excruciating headache caused by the sudden drop in spinal fluid. But nothing could lessen the pain. The body simply had to readjust. So trying not to grind her teeth, she waited for the pain to subside.

The next morning Dr. Martin, who had not been there the night before, came to see how she was doing. At the sight of his familiar sympathetic face, Pann burst into tears. She wanted so much to express her frustration and anger, but she still couldn't speak.

The doctor took her hand and said, "Go ahead and cry. I know what you must be feeling. If you could, you'd get up out of this bed and start running and never come back."

Pann was touched by his compassion. He *did* know how she felt! That fact helped her face the reality that she couldn't run away or escape from what was happening. She was just going to have to live a day at a time and do what needed to be done to survive.

During the next couple of days, Pann was put through more tests. Because her heart continued to race, the cardiologist was called in again. He decided a cardiac coronary angiogram was needed. The procedure required that a catheter be inserted through an artery and run up into the heart. Then dye would be injected so the structure of the heart could be seen. This would give them a clearer picture of what shape Pann's valves were in. But the risks were serious. The procedure could induce another stroke or a heart attack.

Bill and Pann prayed before signing the consent papers. The procedure scared them, but they could see no alternative. They *had* to find out what was wrong.

On Thursday Pann was moved into the intermediate-care unit and hooked up to a heart monitor. The angiogram was scheduled for Monday afternoon.

A cardiac lab is an awesome and frightening place, with its huge machinery and instruments that look like something out of *Star Wars*. Even the special curved table that puts the patient in a half-sitting position looks like something NASA ordered. Pann looked around her cautiously. She wanted to see what was being done, but she didn't want to see *too* much. They weren't going to put her to sleep for the procedure, but they gave her a drug to help her relax. Anxiously she watched them numb her right arm and thread the catheter up the artery. The sensation was strange but not painful.

Everything went well until, suddenly, Pann's heart went wild. She immediately became light-headed and heard herself say, "Hey, Doc, you wouldn't let me check out on you, would you?"

The doctor replied in a deliberately casual tone, "Why, no, Pann." Then he turned and started barking out orders like a drill sergeant. The room became a beehive of activity as everyone rushed to their assigned jobs. Lidocaine was injected directly into the catheter, and within minutes Pann's heart began to slow down. As the beats eased back to a reasonable rate, so did the tension in the lab. Everyone took a deep breath and settled down to complete the test.

A few minutes later, as the dye was injected into Pann's heart, she was instantly aware of an intense sensation of heat sweeping through her body like a forest fire. She had never felt anything like it. Even her eyebrows seemed to perspire, and her toenails felt as if they were going to split.

Perhaps the procedures were rushed because of the way Pann's heart had reacted. But the doctors, who managed to discover that *both* the mitral and tricuspid valves had a significant prolapse, failed to find the patent foramen ovale that would be observed years later at Cedars. How much this oversight affected coming events will never be known. Since the doctors firmly believed that what they found could *not* be the cause of Pann's strokes, the heart was ruled out as the culprit. Trusting their expertise, Bill and Pann accepted this evaluation, which set the stage for the next three frustrating years.

Since the heart was no longer suspect, the doctors

continued their attempt to unravel the mystery of Pann's strokes by scheduling a cerebral angiogram. Perhaps she had an *arterial venus malformation*, a congenital abnormality of the blood vessels in the brain. At this point the only way to find out what *was* wrong was to rule out what wasn't.

The angiogram was scheduled for the following Friday, giving Pann a few days to recover and prepare herself for the next invasion of her body. The thought of going through another ordeal like the one she had just survived was far from pleasant, and she battled waves of panic and the feeling of being swept along by an uncontrollable current of events.

Still, there was peace in the midst of the storm. Bill's parents gave Pann a copy of the *New English Bible,* and she loved it. The updated vocabulary brought new clarity to passages that had once seemed obscure, while giving fresh meaning to others that had always touched her. She read it every chance she got. Since her speech had returned, she found herself frequently sharing its riches with the doctors and nurses, who were intrigued by her enthusiasm.

Yet there is a fine line between applying God's promises and using our Christianity as a mask to hide our true feelings and fears. Pann wanted to be a good witness, and there was nothing insincere about her professions of faith. But she was also experiencing anger and hurt that she didn't feel comfortable expressing. It was easier to ignore or deny them than to risk letting others see what she considered to be chinks in her spiritual armor. She was like a child trying to learn to swim— not in the calm of a swimming pool, but amidst swirling currents and crashing waves. Her victorious Christian façade was her only life preserver, and she dared not let go of it for fear of going under. Eventually that life preserver would become a weight that would drag her to the bottom.

On Friday, Pann steeled herself for another ordeal. At least she would be asleep for this test, something for which she was profoundly grateful, for this time the catheters were to be inserted through the large arteries in her neck.

She awoke in the intermediate-care unit with an extremely sore and swollen neck. The next hours passed in an uncomfortable haze as she drifted in and out of sleep. Then, as though to finish the day with an exclamation point, Pann's heart went wild again, her blood pressure dropped, and she went into shock. She was hurriedly put on IVs and flooded with fluids. Her head was tilted down to raise her blood pressure. By evening the emergency had passed and she was out of danger.

"Can't you do anything the easy way?" Bill teased, his eyes bright with tears of relief, when he came to visit the next morning.

"You know me. Anything for attention." Pann smiled wanly. "Gotta keep these doctors on their toes."

"And you're just the one to do it, too!" Bill walked to the bed and gave his wife a kiss, trying not to wince at the sight of her swollen purple neck. "Very attractive. I always thought you should wear more purple. Does it hurt a lot?"

"Not as much as my arm," Pann said. "I don't understand it. Why should my arm hurt when it's my neck that was assaulted?"

Two days later, as the pain in her arm continued to intensify, Pann learned the answer to that question. By the time Bill arrived on Sunday afternoon, the pain was so severe she had to request a painkiller. Even then the only way Pann was halfway comfortable was to bend the arm at the elbow with her hand raised in the air.

As the afternoon wore on, Pann noticed her lower arm was feeling cooler than the rest of her body, a phenomenon she found curious but not alarming. But the fact that a string of doctors kept coming to examine the arm, walking out without comment, seemed unusual and strangely ominous. She wished that Dr. Martin weren't away for the weekend and that someone would explain what was happening.

Around six that evening Pann's cardiologist walked into the room. "Hi, Toots," he greeted her warmly. He examined her arm with great gentleness and concern. He was a young man, good looking, but known around the hospital for his cool, aloof manner. Pann was surprised and even a little disturbed by his uncharacteristic tenderness. Even the nurse raised an eyebrow in surprise. Finally, he shook his head and announced with regret, "I am so sorry, but we're going to have to call in a surgeon. There is a blood clot in there, and we have to get it out."

"Another blood clot? In my arm?" Pann shot Bill a look of agonized disbelief. What else could possibly go wrong? Bill in turn looked at the doctor, who explained somewhat hesitantly that during the cerebral angiogram they had reopened the incision in Pann's arm and attempted to use the same artery that had been used for the cardiac angiogram five days before. The catheter would not go up that artery, and they had finally closed it, going up the neck arteries, as Pann and Bill had agreed and understood they were going to do in the first place. The result was that the artery in her arm had been traumatized, causing clotting that cut off all circulation to the lower arm.

Pann: "I may have had grounds for a malpractice suit. But at the time I was in such a dependent state, needing my doctors to help me survive and needing to cling to the belief that they knew what they were doing, that I resisted any thought of pressing the point. But there is no question that bad judgment was used, and it almost cost me my arm.

"After the cardiologist saw me, he ordered that I not be served dinner and immediately called in a surgeon. In the

57

meantime I just lay there, writhing in the most excruciating pain imaginable. My arm was literally dying.

"If there is one thing I have learned through my years in hospitals, it is how slow they are to respond to situations like this. One would think that just by looking at my arm and seeing my symptoms they would have known right away what was wrong, but it took nearly two days before anything was done. After being conditioned by television and movies to the image of caring, discerning, and responsive doctors and nurses, it is extremely disillusioning to be faced with reality. I mean, where is Dr. Welby when you really need him?

"On television the doctor walks in, takes one look, diagnoses the problem, orders the appropriate medicine or operation, and by the end of the hour the patient is cured. In real life there are rarely any instant answers. Instead it feels like everything happens in slow motion, especially when you are in great pain. Often nobody appears to be terribly concerned or know what to do. And a lot of times things go wrong with people and the doctors never figure out what's wrong.

"The problem lies on both sides of this issue. On the one hand, physicians are many times too slow and cautious in fear of malpractice suits. On the other hand, we have been sold a bill of goods about the all-knowing doctor, so that we put them on pedestals of perfection and probably expect far too much."

About seven that evening, the doctor called Bill to tell him to come back to the hospital. They were going to have to operate that night if the arm was to be saved.

VII

THE NIGHTMARISH QUALITY of the next few hours intensified every minute. Pann was hastily prepared for surgery and wheeled into the operating room. As the doors swung shut behind her, locking her into the cold, sterile world of the OR, she yearned for the sting of the needle that would bring blessed release from her physical and emotional pain. What a relief the dark, peaceful nothingness would be after the horror of discovering that part of her body was literally dying.

But instead of putting Pann to sleep, the anesthesiologist took one look at her chart, noted that she had gone into shock after her general anesthesia two days before, and decided that putting her under again so soon was too great a risk. To Pann's horror, he opted for a local anesthetic.

At 8:30 P.M. they started injecting novocaine all around the area. Dr. Kohl, the young surgeon, walked in wearing a Budweiser skullcap. At the sight of him, Pann went on a verbal rampage.

"Why don't you put me to sleep?" she demanded. "I don't want to be awake. Please! Why are you doing this to me? I can't stand this. Don't you understand? I want to be asleep. I need to . . . must sleep . . . !" Pann went on and on, totally out of control and drifting farther and farther from reality. At one point she spotted Dr. Kohl's skullcap and cried out, "Don't touch me! You must be drunk! You have Budweiser on your head!"

Pann watched apprehensively as a screen was placed around her head to cut off her view of the procedure, which entailed sending a special probe down the artery to remove the clot. It was a slow, tedious process, and several times Pann had to let them know she was getting some feeling back in her arm and needed more novocaine. She also received periodic injections of morphine to help the pain as the minutes dragged by. Nine-thirty. Ten-thirty . . .

But morphine could not deaden her psychological agony. By eleven-thirty, nearly three hours after the operation had begun, Pann was at the end of her ability to cope. Emotionally she was drained and teetering like Humpty-Dumpty before his fall. In the morning she might still have an arm, but she was sure the rest of her would be little more than a pile of scrambled eggs.

Then, at the point of her greatest despair, God did what the doctors dared not do: He put her to sleep. Pann felt the panic lift, her body relax, and her eyes grow heavy. She remained peacefully asleep through the last and most sensitive part of the surgery. Later she would awake from this little miracle with renewed assurance that even in the midst of this horror, she was not alone or forgotten.

While Pann fought her battle in the OR, Bill faced his own in the quiet of the small chapel. He sat on the hard wooden pew with his head in his hands, feeling like a punch-drunk boxer wondering where that last blow had come from.

Until now, Bill had coped well with Pann's misfortunes. The first stroke had been shocking, but not devastating. But this second stroke and its complications had suddenly and violently catapulted him out of the world of the safe and reasonable, into an alien realm of fear and uncertainty.

His head spun with a million unanswered questions. What was happening? How could things get out of hand like this? And most importantly, *why* was it happening? And why to Pann, of all people? Pann, who was always the first one there if a friend was in need. Pann, who didn't have a mean or rebellious bone in her body. Pann, about whom Paul Kilian had written a few days before:

> I admire you for having the courage to be what I am not and for being willing to pay the price. I've always thought of you as the shining light around these parts. I always looked forward to your comments when we were in prayer group together. You have a remarkable insight into the heart of things, and a beautiful way of coming across. Your cooking is superb; so is your art work; so is your laugh!

Pann had been deeply touched by Paul's letter, and Bill had felt a warm pride that his good friend held his wife in such high esteem. But now Paul's words came back to haunt him as he wrestled with the obvious and frightening questions they raised. How long would it be before he would come home to be greeted by the tempting aroma of Pann's good cooking or find one of her funny little cartoon characters greeting him from his lunch napkin or hear the music of Pann's wonderful laugh? How long would it be if she lost her arm?

Bill felt like punching his fist through the back of the pew in front of him. Instead, he mindlessly patted his pockets for the pack of cigarettes he always had close at hand. Feeling the bulge in his breast pocket, he suddenly realized where he was and what he was doing. His hand fell limp between his knees as an overwhelming sense of guilt rose from his gut and filled his throat, constricting the muscles in a choking sensation. It didn't make any sense. *He* was the one who smoked and swore when he got mad and had a constant struggle disciplining his life when it came to reading the Word or having daily prayer times. But here he sat, strong and well, while Pann lay upstairs, sick and hurting.

Bill had never felt so helpless. As he sat in the chapel, he didn't know how to pray. He didn't even know whether he wanted to. Would someone really listen and care? What if the world was right and religion was nothing more than a man-made panacea for problems with no answers? What if he and Pann were alone? Really alone? The question sent a cold shiver through his body.

Bill didn't hear the door open or realize there was someone else in the room until a hand touched his shoulder. "Bill?"

Bill looked up to see Lloyd Ogilvie standing over him. He could not have been more surprised if it had been the angel Gabriel in a flowing white robe. Dr. Ogilvie was the senior pastor at Hollywood Presbyterian Church, and the demands of his ministry, not to mention the size of his congregation, as a general rule made hospital calls impossible. Besides, Pastor Ogilvie was supposed to be away on study leave.

"Dr. Ogilvie! What are you doing here?" Bill asked in amazement. "I thought you were out of town."

"I was, but this afternoon I felt the Lord impress me that I needed to be with you tonight, so I just jumped in the car and came. Is it all right if I sit with you?"

Bill felt the tears slip down his face as he made room on the bench. Nothing had really changed—no miraculous healing or answers to the hard questions—but this simple touch of a friend was all Bill needed to reassure him Someone did indeed hear and care. He and Pann were not alone.

Bill: "I had been trained to be a Christian. I knew what a Christian was and I loved Jesus. But the close, day-to-day relationship with the Lord wasn't there. Yet the Lord supported me, even though I didn't support Him. I wasn't doing all the 'right' things, yet He carried me. I didn't pray for someone to help me. Still, God sent Lloyd Ogilvie to the hospital that night and later gave me Paul Kilian as a sounding board for my fears and frustrations.

"Over the past years I've had to accept that there is good and bad in this world and that Christ never said He would spare us. What He *did* say was that He would be with us: that He'd never forsake us. And He has kept His promise."

Pann woke up in recovery to find her right arm bound across her chest. When Dr. Kohl walked in a few minutes later, he immediately reassured her. "You're all right. The arm's probably going to be fine. But the clotting was so extensive that we couldn't get it all. We finally had to remove three inches of artery. Now don't panic!" he added quickly. "Arteries stretch and eventually you should be able to straighten the arm. But it will take time and hard work."

The weeks to follow proved just how true those words were. Pann's right arm had already been severely weakened by the second stroke, and it would take five long months of rehabilitation and stretching before her arm could be extended fully. But her arm was not the only thing that would take time to heal. Lying in the intensive-care unit the week after her surgery, Pann experienced a growing panic. The brain test had revealed nothing unusual. For all their trouble, the doctors were no closer to an answer than they had been before.

Pann began to see her illness as a great menacing monster, lying in wait in the dark to devour her—a monster with no face or name, a monster against which she was helpless to defend herself.

Pann: "It epitomized the worst kind of childhood nightmare of being totally at the mercy of something malevolent and evil, which I felt powerless to repel. This was also the beginning of a real fear of just what the future might hold. I'd had two strokes and nobody knew why, or how to keep me from having more.

"A real conflict began in my soul because I had grown up believing, more or less, that as long as I was good and did what I should, God would protect me and make things all right. It wasn't that I didn't have an understanding of Jesus as Savior. I did. I was just totally unprepared for this kind of testing and warfare."

Once again Pann began the long, monotonous weeks of rehabilitation, treating her plants to warm prune juice in the morning, doing combat with her hairbrush, and claiming a great victory for every inch of movement she recovered. At first motivation came hard. After all, she had just made a long, hard climb up the mountain, only to be hurled back down even further than before. But every time she was tempted to give up, she'd think of K.C. and ache with the desire to bury her nose in the silver-blond curls at the nape of his neck and smell the sweetness of baby powder on his soft skin. Perhaps Bill could learn to live with an invalid wife, but K.C. would be walking soon and needed a mother who could hold him and chase after him and push him on a swing. She had to get well for K.C.

This truth was brought home with devastating force when Pann and K.C. were reunited several weeks after her hospitalization. Pann's mother had come down from Seattle to care for her grandson, and she had done her best to keep Pann updated on every new sound or movement. But hearing about K.C. wasn't the same as seeing and holding him. So on the day of K.C.'s first visit, Pann could hardly lie still as she waited for Bill to bring him into the room.

"Are you sure I look all right?" she asked nervously, looking at her mother and Bill's parents, who were there to share the happy occasion.

"You look fine," they all chorused for the third time in five minutes.

Finally Bill walked through the door, proudly carrying his son. Every eye in the room was glued to Pann's shining face as she reached out her good arm to touch him. "Hello, K.C. It's Mommy."

Bill laid the little boy at Pann's side. But darling, happy K.C.—who until that moment had never met anyone he didn't like—took one look at Pann and let out a howl, reaching desperately for his dad.

Horror-stricken, Pann tried to comfort him, awkwardly patting him and trying to keep his straining body from falling off the bed—an impossible task with only one good arm. "Honey, it's all right. It's me, Mommy. Oh, K.C., please don't cry. Mommy loves you."

Helplessly, Pann looked at Bill, who had no choice but to retrieve the screaming child and carry him out of the room. Shaken and embarrassed, everyone quickly followed, leaving Pann and her mother alone.

"Oh, darling, I'm so sorry!" her mother stammered. "He didn't mean it. It's just this strange place and all the commotion. K.C. loves you. You know that. Pann? Are you listening?"

Pann sat immobilized. Tears streamed down her cheeks. Her body was racked with sobs so deep they hadn't yet broken the surface.

"Oh, honey, it'll be all right. I promise." Eileen Langford gathered her daughter into her arms and prayed that somehow God would transfer the pain from Pann's fragile body to her own. How often she had prayed that prayer as she sat watching her child suffer these last few weeks. Yet somehow this pain of the soul and heart was even more unbearable, for as a mother, she knew that nothing cut more deeply than being rejected by one's own child.

"He didn't know me, Mother," Pann wailed. "My own baby was afraid of me! Oh, what am I going to do? What have I done to make God hate me so? Tell me! What?"

Mrs. Langford gently rocked her daughter, as she had done when Pann was a child, and softly crooned words of comfort in her ear. How often had King David spoken similar words in the Psalms? "My God, my God, why have you forsaken me? Why do you refuse to help me or even to listen to my groans?" (Psalm 22:1 LB).

Yet that same David would write in Psalm 30:2–5, "O Lord my God, I called to you for help and you healed me. O Lord, you brought me up from the grave; you spared me from going down into the pit. Sing to the Lord, you saints of his; praise his holy name. For his anger lasts only a moment, but his favor lasts a lifetime; weeping may remain for a night, but rejoicing comes in the morning."

There are times when the darkness of the night seems impenetrable and unending, when the only thing to do is to hold on and keep walking in faith, one step at a time, trusting and believing, despite all evidence to the contrary, that God loves us and is working His will to our good and His glory. Hard as it was, all Mrs. Langford could do was hold Pann as she fought to rise above this last unexpected blow. The tears had to be shed and the anger and hurt had to be voiced. But in the morning there would be new strength and determination to face this thing that separated Pann from those she loved—and a new will to conquer it.

VIII

ANN REREAD the journal entry she had written two days
before.

October 7, 1975

Some of my deepest fears became reality in July when I
suffered a second stroke. During a long and eventful
hospitalization, many tests were done to find the cause of
my illness. But after the results were in, even the very best
doctors were at a loss to explain what was wrong, and I was
overcome by an awe of the mystery of God's creation.

I have come to a deep conviction of God's true power
and dominion and goodness, and am convinced that He
does not cause the bad in our lives. He did not cause my
strokes. I am also convinced that He could have, by virtue
of His rule and power, prevented my illness if He chose, just
as He could have sent thirty legions of angels to take His
own Son off the cross. But since He did not choose to
prevent my strokes, I feel certain that He means for *real*

good to come out of them, as fantastic good came of the agony of the cross. So I surrender myself to His will and thank Him for giving me peace.

Pann had a faintly quizzical smile on her face. What would other people think of her words, knowing all she had gone through? Would they call her a super saint, a fool, or an idealist who hid her fears and resentments behind high-sounding rhetoric? Perhaps she was a little of all those, for Pann was discovering that one of the miracles of life and survival is the many different emotional resources God provides when we are required to bear the unbearable and accept the unacceptable.

With deliberate and studied effort, Pann stretched out her right arm, flexed her fingers, and noted with satisfaction that she could almost straighten her elbow. In the past eight months, life had been stripped to its basics: the instinctive struggle to survive and the determination to recover quickly and fully. Everything else had been swept away, like so much dust in the corners, leaving an air of fresh orderliness about her life. Pann felt acutely aware of what was and was not important.

Now, curled on the living-room couch, looking out the window at the rain-soaked street and gray unfriendly sky, Pann felt a pleasant shiver of contentment. Warm and cozy, she listened to the patter of raindrops on the roof. Like a boat anchored safely at harbor, she was sheltered from the buffeting winds and raging seas. A profound sense of quiet came over her spirit as she sat in the comfort of her home with her baby peacefully asleep in his bed. The afternoon stretched lazily before her, free from immediate worries or fears. Oh, the monster was still out there in the darkness, but she no longer felt his breath on her neck. And the distance between them made it possible for her to relax and contemplate.

She balanced her journal on her knees and reached for a yellow marker. On a clean page she drew a large question mark and wrote:

Today I sit with peace in the midst of a life marked by a question mark. We have come to the end of the road in terms of brain tests, and we still have no answer to explain what has caused my strokes and continues to cause my visual problems. But I am grateful for God's unfailing love in my life and realize that faith is the prescription I need to have filled daily to live without fear.

Pann smiled as she imagined a nurse coming into her hospital room with a small white medicine cup. "Now here are your faith pills, Pann. Take them like a good girl."

If only faith came that easily, for if Pann had learned anything through the months of uncertainty, it was that faith is the antidote for fear. It is a living thing, sprouting from the seeds of God's Word planted within our hearts and nourished by every new experience of God's faithfulness.

The things I want—clear vision, assurance of no more visual blackouts, and no more strokes—I cannot have. But if I spend my life in fear of those things, I can only lose out on the tremendous joys of each day. The biggest emotional letdown is past, and now I must lean strongly on God's powerful peace to reign each day in my heart.

The Bible is a rich storehouse of comfort. From Revelation I read, "Behold, the tabernacle of God is with men, and he will dwell with them, and they shall be his people. . . . And God shall wipe away all tears from their eyes" (Rev. 21:3–4 KJV). A special promise indeed!

In the fourth Psalm (verse 8 NEB) I am assured with David, who says, "Now I will lie down in peace, and sleep; for thou alone, O Lord, makest me live unafraid." And Psalm 30:11–12 (NEB) is true inspiration in the darkness. "Thou hast turned my laments into dancing; thou hast stripped off my sackcloth and clothed me with joy, that my spirit may sing psalms to thee and never cease. I will confess thee for ever, O Lord my God."

Finishing the quote, Pann paused to search her heart. Did she really believe what she had written? After all, these pages were for her eyes only, meant to log—as one might log a difficult journey into uncharted waters—her honest impressions and discoveries. Her observations would have no value if they didn't indicate precisely where she was and what she was feeling.

Well, Pann reasoned, *there was no question about the question mark.* It hung over her like a twisted halo, perversely declaring the precariousness of her life. But the peace was real too. Not that there weren't times when it slipped away, hovering irritatingly beyond her grasp. But at this moment, in this place, she had peace. And joy! And hope! And faith that tomorrow or the next day or perhaps next week or next month the question mark would be erased and the monster unmasked.

A small, persistent cry broke into Pann's thoughts. K.C. was awake. The afternoon was gone. Pann closed the notebook with a satisfied slap and went to her son.

IX

*'Tis the season of Christmas and all through the
house
Every creature is stirring, yes, even the mouse!
Our spirits are filled with a great jubilation
For together we share in Christ's birth celebration.*

"THAT'S GREAT! I love it!" Bill laughed, reading over his wife's
shoulder as she composed a Christmas poem that she and
Bill would send out in place of greeting cards. He read on:

*Our K.C. is growing by leaps and by bounds.
He walks and he talks and with smiles abounds.
In professor-type glasses he's a great-looking boy
Whose sweet gentle nature is to us a real joy.*

Since K.C. had celebrated his first birthday and taken his
first steps, life had been one merry chase. It was as if K.C.'s
motto was "Why walk when you can run?" His antics kept his

parents in a constant state of delighted exhaustion. His "professor-type" glasses (a corrective measure until surgery could be performed to strengthen his weak eye muscles) only added to his comic charm. When caught doing something that was a definite no-no, all he had to do was peer innocently over the rims with one of his astonished "Who, me?" looks to send his parents into helpless laughter.

Laughter, music, and optimism filled the Baltz home. As Pann went on to express in her Christmas poem, Bill was doing well at work. His team of workers at Xerox were consistently rated at the top—a miracle, considering the emotional and mental demands he had faced over the past months. He was also, to quote Pann, "a deacon at church and has gained a reputation / as a dependable man for sick visitation!"

Another great blessing for which Pann and Bill were particularly grateful was the overwhelming loyalty and concern of so many friends. The selfless giving of family members such as Pann's mom and her cousin Phyllis was deeply appreciated. But many *others* had offered their time and help, not just once or twice, but frequently over the long months. Paul and Gloria Kilian; Pann's other prayer partner, Darlene Kostrub; and K.C.'s godmother, Melody—all had volunteered to take care of K.C. during Pann's hospitalizations and then pitched in when she came home. During these months of recovery, Gloria, Darlene, and Melody had taken turns coming to the house to do what Pann still could not manage alone—which was, at first, just about everything.

For Pann, all the loving help was not easy to accept. She had always been a giver, believing wholeheartedly the Bible's dictum that it is more blessed to give than to receive. Now she was learning it's also *easier* to give than to receive. Being unable to take care of her son, do her own cooking, and keep her own house was humbling. An overwhelming sense of helplessness would at times send her into moods that were not pleasant or easy to be around. Yet never once did these dear friends threaten to abandon ship. They loved Pann and understood that her impatience was with her own disability and did not reflect a lack of love or appreciation for their contributions.

But these women were merely the spearhead of a whole force of friends "far and near / who have prayed or have written or have sent dinners here."

"So . . . ," Pann finished her Christmas greeting,

> We sing with those angels and rejoice greatly here
> For the gift of life we've been given this year.
> And we wish you this Christmas a glorious day
> In your loving celebration of Jesus' birthday!

Celebration! That is what Christmas 1975 promised to be. The past ten months had been a nightmare from which Pann and Bill had prayed to awaken. On these bright, crisp December days, with Christmas carols and the smell of pumpkin bread and cookies filling the house, it was easy to believe their prayers had been answered.

As Bill put the finishing touches on the Christmas tree, he called Pann in for a final inspection.

"Oh, it's beautiful! The best ever!" Pann exclaimed. "What do you think, K.C.?"

K.C. stood wide-eyed with wonder, surveying the glittering tangle of colored balls, lights, and tinsel. At first he seemed uncertain how to respond. Then with slow, tentative steps, he approached the tree and reached out a dimpled hand to touch a sparkling bauble on a branch. He studied the tree for several long seconds, peering over his dark-rimmed glasses. Then, looking back over his shoulder at his parents' expectant faces, he broke into a wide grin and began giggling and jabbering with delight.

Bill too was caught up in the spirit of the holidays and the hope of the new year. For a while thinking about the future had been difficult. Pann's condition had been too uncertain. The doctors had been noncommittal about how much function her arm would recover, and Bill had tried to prepare himself for the possibility that Pann might be severely disabled. But her will to recover and to reclaim every possible fraction of movement had produced miraculous results, so much so that Bill had decided to reward her with a special Christmas surprise.

Ever since they were married, Pann had yearned to own a piano. She loved music and was an accomplished pianist. After her arm surgery, there was serious doubt that Pann would ever regain the strength and coordination to play again. But she had made such terrific progress that Bill was certain Pann would prove the doubters wrong. And playing would be great therapy.

On the day before Christmas Bill sent Pann on some errands to ensure her absence for a couple of hours. During that time, a truck pulled up in front of the house to deliver a beautiful console piano. Bill had the movers put it in the dining room; then he covered it with a blanket in an attempt to camouflage what was underneath. He topped the whole thing with a bouquet of ribbons and then went into the living room to await Pann's return.

As he paced and listened for the sound of her car in the drive, Bill found himself fluctuating between tears and a big Cheshire-cat grin. How good God was! They had made it through all the pain and misery, and now Pann was even going to have her music! Bill didn't make a habit of praying out loud, but he was overwhelmed by God's faithfulness. "Thank You, Lord," he said in a husky whisper.

When Pann arrived, her delight was everything Bill had hoped for. She immediately sat down and began to stroke the keys lovingly. K.C.'s touch was more heavy-handed, but his happy bangs echoed his mother's joy in the special gift.

That evening, family members gathered to celebrate Jesus' birthday, and the house rang with music and laughter. Pann served baked ham with all the trimmings. After dinner, they gathered in front of the fireplace, where Bill read the Christmas story from Luke. Then they all went off to church for a special midnight service.

In bed that night, Pann was almost dizzy with exhaustion, but it had been worth it! "I can't remember a more wonderful Christmas Eve or a more wonderful present. Thank you for the piano. It means so much to me," Pann said, snuggling under Bill's arm.

"The pleasure's all mine, believe me!" Bill answered. Then he playfully added, "And just think, Santa hasn't even come yet. We still have tomorrow to look forward to."

"Well, I already got what I wanted," Pann replied sleepily.

"Me too, Mouse. Me too." He gently kissed the top of her head and gave his Christmas present an extra squeeze.

Christmas morning passed in a happy flurry of stockings and presents. Although he was too young to fully understand, K.C. soon got into the spirit of things, happily tearing open one present after another, only to discard the gift in favor of the brightly colored paper and ribbons.

"Oh, if only he could stay so easy to please," Pann observed with a laugh as her son buried himself in a pile of rumpled paper.

"Don't count on it. In another year or two he'll have a Christmas list a mile long!" Bill said as he started to clean up the mess. "Better get ready. My folks are expecting us."

Pann stood up a little shakily and waited for a slight dizziness to pass. She felt tired and knew she was pushing, but didn't everyone do that on Christmas? Tomorrow she would rest. Right now she needed to get dressed, get K.C. ready, and fix her special sweet-potato dish to take for Christmas dinner.

Later, as she hurried to put the finishing touches on her

casserole, Pann was aware of feeling off-balance, as if the kitchen floor were tilted. She constantly grabbed the sink to steady herself. Still, she didn't give the feeling much thought, attributing it to exhaustion.

"You ready, Pann?" Bill called as he carried the last box of presents to the car.

Pann quickly gave her house one final inspection. She hated to leave things a mess. She was a fastidious housekeeper, and one of the irritations of her illness had been not having things exactly as she wanted them at all times. Now she checked to make sure everything was clean and in place, so when she came home, she could just relax.

"Come on, Pann!" Bill called from the car where he and K.C. waited.

"Coming!" Pann picked up the dish of sweet potatoes and headed toward the car. As she pulled the door closed behind her, she again felt strangely off-balance. Walking to the car was like walking a tightrope, each foot carefully placed in front of the other. She felt as though she were a drunk trying to walk a straight line. She made it without incident and gratefully plopped down in the front seat. She considered saying something to Bill, but one look at his carefree, happy face made her decide against it. After all, she was just tired. It was nothing to make a big deal over.

Bill turned the car radio on, and the air immediately rang with the joyful news, "Joy to the world, the Lord is come!" Pann leaned her head back against the seat, trying to relax and just float on the music. But as the minutes passed, she became more and more disoriented. She felt as though she were losing herself. It became an effort to stay connected to the world around her, to see, to speak. Suddenly she was frightened. This had gone too far, and now she didn't have the strength to fight it.

"Bill." She mouthed the word and was horrified to realize

nothing had come out. "Bill!" she cried out in a panic to communicate. "I'm sick! I'm really sick!"

Bill turned to see his wife looking at him with a glazed, panicked expression on her ashen face. All this time he had thought she was sleeping, resting up for the day ahead. Instead, the nightmare was beginning again.

"Pann? It's all right. I'll get you to the hospital." Bill steered the car off the freeway and pulled over to the side, to take a better look at Pann. Her body was slumped against the door. He feverishly rubbed her hands and patted her cheek, but she did not respond.

He felt her neck for a pulse. *She's dead!* he thought for one frozen moment. Then, after what seemed a lifetime, he became aware of a faint but steady beat.

"Thank God," Bill breathed, throwing the car into gear and heading for the hospital. He had no thoughts, no prayers, no cries—just an awareness that, with K.C. in the car, he had to drive carefully. All other emotions had drained from Bill's body.

X

I DON'T KNOW how much more of this I can take," Bill said to Paul Kilian as they sat in the Kilian's living room. It had been over a week since Pann's third stroke. "I feel so helpless and angry. And the worst of it is, I have this great anger against Pann. I know it sounds terrible. It doesn't make sense. She's a victim. But I'm a victim too, and so is K.C. Our entire life together has been turned upside down by this thing, and there's nothing we can do!"

Paul listened, nodding occasionally, but did not say much. He knew Bill needed to air his thoughts and emotions to someone who wouldn't pretend to have all the answers or pass judgment on feelings that might not sound noble or pretty, but which were, nonetheless, honest and needed to be dealt with.

"I keep asking myself just how it will end," Bill continued. "I've realized that we're not going to wake up one day and find our lives back to normal and everything okay. Pann may *never* be okay, and the idea tears me up inside. I love her, Paul, and I hate seeing her like this. I've actually found myself wondering if it wouldn't be better for Pann if the Lord took her home. Then I feel guilty for thinking it. I mean, who am I kidding? Better for Pann? What I *mean* is better for me! Easier. Simpler. Pann dies and my life goes back to normal, free from hospitals and doctors and pain and fear—the constant fear! I can't even sleep anymore. No matter how tired I am, a part of me won't relax. It stays alert and listens for the phone to ring announcing that something else bad has happened!"

Bill could feel his fingernails biting into the palms of his hands. "Sometimes I wish I had the courage to just walk away from the whole mess." His voice was barely more than a whisper. "I mean, this isn't what life's supposed to be all about. I hate it! I resent it! I want my wife back, healthy and whole. I want my life back! Then, when I think about how much Pann has suffered, I despise myself for being so weak and selfish."

Bill's voice went flat and his body relaxed. He ran his fingers through his hair and rubbed his eyes in a gesture of exhaustion. "Oh, I don't know. I'm just so tired. I'm not making sense."

"No, you're making a lot of sense," Paul said. "Most people would feel the same way in your situation. They just wouldn't be honest enough to admit it." Paul stood up to throw another log on the fire, then turned to study the dejected figure slumped on the couch. The log suddenly caught fire, casting flickering shadows that played off the planes and hollows of Bill's exhausted face.

"You know, Bill, you're going to make it through whatever lies ahead. You have nothing to be ashamed of. Gloria and I have watched you this past year with amazement. We've been touched by your loyalty and strength. I mean, look at this thing honestly. Like you said, your whole life has been turned upside down. If someone had asked us before how you would manage under these circumstances, we would have had our doubts."

Paul continued, choosing his words carefully, "You and Pann married with very definite ideas of what you wanted marriage to be and the roles you both wanted to play. You had specific demands you wanted met, and at first it seemed as if you'd found the perfect mate to meet those demands. But this past year has broken all the rules, and now you're faced with having to throw the rule book away completely and start living by an entirely new one—one that says that there *are* no rules, no set patterns, no guarantees. That would be enough to send many men scurrying for cover, looking for a way out. But you've been a constant source of strength and comfort to Pann— holding down a difficult job; stopping here after work every day to make sure K.C. is all right and taking him to see Pann when possible; going to the hospital every evening, no matter how tired you are; and taking care of K.C. full-time on weekends. Boy, I don't mind telling you, we worried about that one! Neither Gloria nor I had ever seen you change a diaper or fix a bottle, yet look at you now! You're every bit as good a "mommy" as you are a daddy.

"What I'm trying to say," Paul said, moving to the couch where Bill sat, "is that we're proud of you. We see all you've been through and know Pann's not the only one suffering. More than that, God sees and knows."

Bill stared into the fire, tears running down his cheeks. It was good to hear someone say he was all right. He desperately needed the reassurance that he wasn't a bad guy because he had an occasional weak moment or ugly thought.

Gloria walked into the room with a tray of steaming mugs and said, "I thought you guys might like some coffee. How's Pann doing?" She settled in a chair next to the fireplace.

"Okay, all things considered. The stroke is over, and

they're going to move her to rehab tomorrow," Bill answered, gratefully sipping the hot brew.

"So soon?" Gloria asked in surprise. "That seems awfully quick."

"They don't know what else to do. She's already had every test in the book. It's like they've thrown up their hands and said, 'We give up. We don't know what's wrong. Let's just get her rehabilitated and send her home as soon as possible, and let's hope it doesn't happen again.' At least that's how it feels to us. I think Pann is beginning to feel they have given up on her, and it scares her. It scares me too," Bill admitted. "After all, when the doctors stop trying, what's left?"

"A miracle," suggested Gloria. "You mustn't give up hope."

"I'm trying not to," Bill answered, "but sometimes it's hard. This stroke has been by far the most damaging. It could take months before she'll be able to speak clearly. And you know Pann; not being able to talk is the ultimate frustration!"

Paul and Gloria both smiled, remembering how much Pann liked to chat. "That brings to mind something else that's been bothering me. . . ." Bill's voice trailed off. The Kilians waited for him to continue. "The doctors seem to be exploring the possibility that Pann's problem is not physical."

"You mean they think all this may be in her head?" Paul asked incredulously.

"At this point they're willing to consider any possibility. They have no other answers. They're grasping at straws. Of course, Pann was outraged by the suggestion, and I don't blame her. The idea that she has somehow brought all this on herself is really the final blow. I don't think I've ever seen her spirits so low."

"Well, at least she knows you don't believe that," Gloria responded.

"No, I don't—not really—but something strange did happen the day I admitted her to the hospital. I haven't told anyone, not even Pann, but it's really eating away at me. After I took Pann up to her room and she was settled in bed, I could swear I heard her say clear as day, 'I can't talk.' Just like that: 'I can't talk.' I know it sounds crazy. She had lost her speech completely by that time and was barely conscious. Yet I was almost certain I heard her speak. I have to admit, it made me wonder."

The room fell silent as the three friends sipped their coffee and watched the flames dance in the fireplace. No one spoke. No one had an answer.

XI

FOR PANN, the next weeks of rehabilitation were the most difficult of her ordeal to date. Each day, she spent hours in speech therapy, reteaching her lips and tongue to work together to form the most basic sounds and words. It was a slow, trying process, which required hours of repetition. With the additional physical therapy needed to restore the use of her right arm and leg, Pann's days were full and exhausting.

While Pann gave herself to her therapy with characteristic determination, an uncharacteristic gloom hovered over her like a dark cloud. It cast a shadow over all her efforts and sent her into frequent bouts of depression. How long would her recovery take this time? If the doctors had given up hope of finding a cure, what did the future hold? Why should she work to get strong again if the same thing was going to keep happening?

At one point, Pann began to question whether winning the war was worth the pain and struggle of each battle. Nighttime was the worst. Tormenting thoughts came to her, lodged stubbornly in her mind, and repeated like a broken record. She thought of her new piano, which a short time ago had symbolized the joyful possibilities of the future, sitting untouched and silent. Now it was a monument to the fleeting months of hope they had enjoyed. And the Christmas poem she had composed, giving God the praise for having brought them through a dark and difficult year. The sense of somehow having lost God's protective covering was the hardest thing to face. What had she done? Why didn't God heal her once and for all? And if He wasn't going to heal her, why didn't He let her die?

As the weeks passed, Pann's condition improved and her spirits rose. The only persistent symptom was a sparkling effect in her vision. The doctors decided to treat her with Dilantin, a medication used to control hemiplegic migraines. The Dilantin did help clear Pann's vision, but she experienced a minor allergic reaction to the drug and broke out in a rash. After the rash disappeared within a few days, the doctors felt it was safe to continue the medicine.

As the time of Pann's release approached, she had mixed emotions about going home. She missed Bill and K.C. and wanted nothing more than to walk out of that hospital without looking back. But going home with all her disabilities was not easy. Once again she would be dependent upon others to do all the things she couldn't. And each hospital stay left her more insecure about herself as a woman. How could Bill not be turned off by all the scars on her body and the awkwardness of her movement and speech? Pann saw nothing appealing about herself, and her self-doubt made going home a mixed blessing.

Since patients with long-term traumatic illnesses often have difficulty returning home, the hospital's policy was to send them home for weekend visits to help ease them back into the world they had left so abruptly. Pann made two such visits home before her release. The first weekend home she was covered with the rash from her Dilantin reaction. Spotted and itching, she gained little confidence from that visit. By the next weekend, however, the rash was gone, and her stay was so happy and encouraging that it was difficult to return to the hospital. Pann comforted herself with the knowledge that when she came home the following weekend, it would be for good!

During that last week in rehabilitation, Pann threw herself into therapy with even more energy to accomplish as much as possible before going home. Her progress was good. Although she was still in a wheelchair, she was regaining strength and movement in both her right arm and leg, and her speech was improving daily. The rash had returned, but compared with everything else she had suffered, it was a minor irritation. Still, the doctors were concerned about her continued reaction to Dilantin and decided to take her off it on Thursday.

Finally Friday came. Pann had been in the hospital nearly two months. As she went through her morning routine, she said good-bye to her fellow patients and the therapists, announcing joyfully, "I'm going home tomorrow!" As the morning wore on, Pann became conscious of an irritating tickle in her throat. It felt as if the rash on her body had spread to her throat. By the end of her morning therapy session, she was coughing and feeling out of breath. The therapist who helped her back to her room asked if Pann was having trouble breathing.

Pann nodded, too out of breath to answer. The nurse immediately called for a respiratory therapist. Oxygen equipment was rushed into the room, and Pann's nose and mouth were covered by an oxygen mask. Despite the help, her labored breathing soon turned to urgent gasps for air.

"This isn't working," the therapist announced. "She's going into stridor. [Stridor occurs when throat tissue swells, obstructing the air passage to the lungs.] We'd better call Doctor Martin."

By the time Dr. Martin arrived, Pann's gasping was loud and frantic. "I had no idea she was this bad. We need a specialist. Get Doctor Eisenberg here, stat!" he ordered tersely.

The few minutes it took the respiratory specialist to get to her room seemed like an eternity to Pann. She recalls, "Of all the terrifying things I have experienced, not being able to breathe was the most frightening. Death seemed the most imminent. I was literally fighting for my life, taking seventy breaths a minute by the time Doctor Eisenberg arrived. Normally, we take about twenty."

Dr. Eisenberg walked into the room, looking like someone out of a Smith Brother's cough-drop ad. He was tall and balding, with horn-rimmed glasses, a long, scraggly beard, and eyes that wandered in different directions. He was a sight to behold. Picking up Pann's chart, he spoke first to the nurse. "Her name on the chart is Patricia. Is that what she goes by?"

"No," the nurse answered, surprised by the question. "They call her Pann . . . P–a–n–n."

"I see by her history that she's had a stroke. Does she speak? Does she understand?"

The nurse assured him that Pann did.

"Good," he said. It had taken the doctor all of ten seconds to get that information. Now he walked over to the bed and took Pann's hand. "Pann," he said in a firm, calm voice, "I'm Doctor Eisenberg, and I am here to help you. I know you're having trouble breathing, but I don't want you to be afraid. I am going to help you. Now, this place is going to get pretty busy, and I don't want you to worry about what we're doing. You do one thing, and one thing only. You concentrate on breathing and leave the rest to me. I'm going to take care of you, understand? You just worry about getting each breath, and you'll be all right."

It took less than a minute for the doctor to make his little speech, but it was the most effective thing he could have done. He had called Pann by name, touched her, and reassured her that she was not alone. His compassion would always stand out in Pann's memory.

Then Dr. Eisenberg jumped up from the bed and started firing off orders. An IV was started. Different types of breathing equipment were rolled in and then out again, as their ineffectiveness was proven. Amidst all this organized chaos, Pann was amazed to see the concerned face of Pastor Herb Downie of Hollywood Presbyterian Church. Pastor Downie had known Pann since she was a child, and he just happened to be making hospital calls when he heard she was having trouble. Thinking perhaps that his presence might calm her, the doctors allowed him to step into the room for a minute. At the sight of his familiar face, Pann struggled to gasp out one word: "Bill."

"We need to get her husband here," Pastor Downie told the doctor.

Herb Downie's face was Pann's last clear image. People and voices faded in and out as she desperately sucked for air. At some point she heard Dr. Eisenberg shout, "Get a bed in ICU and get ready to roll!"

The trip from rehab at one end of the hospital to the intensive care unit at the other end was much like Mr. Toad's Ride at Disneyland—fast and crazy. People were stationed all along the route, holding doors and elevators open and making sure no one was in the way as Pann's bed was literally run down the halls. The trip, which would normally take five or six minutes, was finished in one. Once she was in the intensive-care unit, the pace became even more frantic. It was obvious to the doctors that Pann was having an anaphylactic drug reaction to the Dilantin. Her throat was swelling shut. If they didn't get some air into her lungs, she would die.

XII

BILL WAS IRRITATED when his beeper went off. He was out in the field with one of his technicians, and they were just finishing one job before going on to another. After that they would be through for the day, unless this call meant another problem.

When he called his office, Bill was informed that Dr. Martin wanted to talk to him. He dialed the hospital, more curious than alarmed. After all, Pann was doing well. She was coming home tomorrow.

"Pann's developed a little trouble with her breathing this afternoon," said the doctor, deliberately wording his statement so as not to panic Bill. "I called in a specialist, and he thought it would be wise to move her up to intensive care so we can keep an eye on her. I think it'd be a good idea for you to come to the hospital."

Disarmed by the doctor's understated tone, Bill asked, "Do you mean after work or now?"

"I think it would be a good idea for you to come now." Dr. Martin wisely kept the urgency out of his voice. There was no sense in Bill racing recklessly to the hospital and possibly having an accident. The way things were going, he might not make it in time, even if he did hurry.

Pann's condition continued to deteriorate. She was given steroids to control the swelling, but the reaction had gone too far. The last thing Pann remembered was someone saying she couldn't breathe by herself and would have to be put on a respirator. The voice explained that they were going to put a tube down her throat, but for Pann the meaning of the words was elusive and strangely unimportant. She was slipping, drifting, disengaging. Suddenly everything went black. She felt as though she were enveloped in a dark velvety tunnel. There was nothing frightening about it. Instead, Pann found her senses marvelously responsive—as if she could touch the darkness.

Pann heard voices and music. Although the voices were unintelligible, Pann found herself listening with fascination, not fear. The music was the most beautiful she had ever heard, like chimes—crystal clear and sweet.

For a moment Pann felt the urge to move toward the music, but thoughts of Bill and K.C. made her pause. Before that moment it had been as if the physical world had ceased to exist. She had felt no sorrow or regret in leaving it. But now she felt an overwhelming desire to go back to her husband and son. She was aware of unfinished business and felt the pull of ties not yet broken.

Abruptly the scene changed. Pann was back in this world, but as an observer, not a participant. Hovering at ceiling level, she watched with detached curiosity as doctors and nurses crowded around a lifeless body on the bed. The body was her own; Pann was free of it. From her vantage point, not only was she able to see everything in the little ICU cubicle, but also all the hubbub outside its glass walls. Dozens of people rushed from one place to another, moved equipment, checked readouts, and shouted orders in a desperate attempt to save her life. In one corner of the next room several doctors whom Pann didn't recognize were deep in discussion. In another corner a respirator and defibrillator were being readied. Suddenly one of the unfamiliar doctors left the group and walked purposefully into the room. Pann saw him approach the table. Then everything went dark as she was gripped by a searing pain that felt like someone had jabbed a hot poker down her throat. In reality it was an intubation tube being inserted down her nose and throat, through her larynx, and into her lungs. Finally she was getting oxygen, but the pain was excruciating.

"Good! She's fighting. We haven't lost her," a voice declared in the hazy distance beyond the pain.

When Bill arrived at the hospital he was unsure of what to expect. *Certainly Dr. Martin would have been more urgent if Pann were in danger,* he told himself as he made his way to the intensive-care unit. Only when the nurse refused to let him in and he was told that a doctor would be out to talk to him did Bill's palms begin to sweat with apprehension.

Finally Dr. Eisenberg came through the doors and introduced himself.

"Doctor Martin called to say Pann is having trouble breathing," Bill began. "How's she doing? Is she better?"

"Better?" Dr. Eisenberg rolled his eyes skyward in a way that would have been comic under different circumstances. "Mr. Baltz, you'd better sit down." Then the doctor explained how close Bill had come to losing his wife. "Now," said Dr. Eisenberg, "I think we've got her stabilized, but we'll have to keep a close eye on her."

For the next few days, Pann's existence was defined by the levels of pain she endured: throbbing, burning, unrelenting waves of it, washing over her and catching her up in their violent ebb and flow. It churned, lashed, sucked her downward. Then the prick of a needle would introduce more morphine into her system and draw her up until her head just broke the surface, allowing her to gasp a few lifesaving breaths before being plunged into the depths once again.

"Pann? Honey, I'm here. What can I do for you? Anything you need? Anything you want?" The questions were rhetorical, spoken out of Bill's desperate need to fight his own helplessness. If only he could *do* something! But there was nothing anyone could do, beyond giving her morphine every few hours. As Dr. Martin explained, morphine isn't always completely effective. In Pann's case, this seemed especially true. Within the first two hours after the breathing tube was inserted, she had been given twenty-five milligrams, about five times the average dose, and she was still in pain.

The morphine, however, did lessen the pain some. As the effect of the previous injection wore off, Pann would look forward to the next friendly sting of the needle. This was Pann's introduction to the seduction of narcotics, and while she didn't become addicted at this time, she learned they could help her temporarily escape her physical and mental torment.

Nearly a week passed before they were able to wean Pann off the respirator. Then she was transferred to the intermediate-care unit to begin the process of healing and rehabilitation once again. The week of intravenous feedings had caused a dramatic weight loss and Pann was so weak that even chewing and swallowing were difficult.

During her days of enforced silence, she could only communicate by awkwardly jotting a few words on paper with her left hand. Obviously this only provided minimal communication and made it impossible for her to express her deeper thoughts and feelings. For instance, the day after her respiratory arrest, a doctor came into her room and introduced himself as the one who had inserted her respiratory tube, thus saving her life.

"I know," wrote Pann. "I saw you."

"But you couldn't have," the doctor replied, perplexed. "You were unconscious."

For a long moment their eyes met, the doctor's questioning, Pann's glazed with pain but direct and unwavering. The doctor was the first to look away, glancing nervously at his watch. "Well," he said, rising to leave, "we'll talk about it another time. I'll be back."

As he walked through the door, Pann longed to call out, "Wait! I want to tell you what happened to me! I need to tell you. I need to tell *someone*." But her thoughts were prisoners, locked in by the burning tube in her throat and guarded by the ever-present pain.

When the tubes were removed, Pann was finally free to talk about her incredible experience. But the words did not come easily. Her thoughts were confused, and the effort of putting them into words was overwhelming. What had happened to her was unique, and it was not easy to share with others what had been a very private and intimate revelation of God's power and reality.

The doctor who saved her life did come back to talk. He nodded in agreement as Pann described what she had seen and heard during the time her spirit was released from the confines of her body. He offered no argument, having accepted long ago that there are mysteries that medical science will never solve or understand.

But the doctor didn't seem to catch the true significance of what Pann was saying. She had left her body. She—that part of her that thought and felt and would exist forever—had taken the first steps toward an eternity that all Christians look to as the great promise of salvation. And she had come back able to testify that it is indeed a reality. She had heard the chimes of heaven. She had heard the voices of the saints praising God and had felt the peace and joy of going home. Thinking about it as she lay in her hospital bed, Pann was convinced that the only reason she had not gone on to complete her journey was because she never saw the Light at the end of the darkness. If she had seen the Light—if she had seen Jesus—nothing could have drawn her back. But God chose not to take her. Instead He sent her back to Bill and K.C. and her parents; back to their love and concern and needs. Back also to an imperfect body racked with pain and the ever-present question mark: why?

No, she had not been miraculously healed or given the answer to her problems, but she had been given something far more valuable: peace in the knowledge that God was in control. He could have taken her home, but He chose not to, and the fact that He sent her back meant He had something for her to do. Her life had meaning, a purpose, and most importantly, a future. That knowledge gave her confidence that God wasn't through with her—not yet. Pann had received another precious gift from this experience: She knew she would never again fear death. She would still have to deal with the fear of pain and the feelings of loss, but she had seen the other side and could declare with the apostle Paul, "Where, O death, is your victory? Where, O death, is your sting?" (1 Corinthians 15:55).

XIII

March 14, 1976

It is a Sunday afternoon, and I sit in the same hospital ward that I sat in one year ago today. The reason for my being here is a third stroke on Christmas Day. I was recovering when I had a violent reaction to a drug being used to help me, and I suffered a respiratory arrest.

I have felt through this hospitalization that there is a book inside of me to be written, God willing. Here I hope to set down the feelings and lessons I've had and learned, to be the material for that book.

First and foremost, I give the glory to God for His answers to prayer and His best healing—the peace within. On the Sunday before Christmas we were at church and some friends from Koinonians asked a question I had not been asked before during this year of turmoil. They said they were praying for me but wanted me to tell them *how* they should pray. Although I had given no thought to that question, the answer came quickly and without hesitation from a heart healed by God.

Don't pray that I won't have another stroke. That's in God's hands and in His will. But do pray that if indeed that is in my future, I can make each day count, so that I can look back without regrets. And that I can be used every day, even in the midst of an illness, should it strike.

It was just four days later that I suffered my third stroke. Every bit of the prayer request I made was answered, really. I look back on the three months I had at home between my second and third strokes and there are no regrets. It was really choice living with K.C. and Bill. Some said when they heard that the third stroke happened on Christmas Day, "Oh, it ruined Christmas!" But I have to say with honesty, "No, it didn't." The morning we shared as a family, giving gifts, thrilling to the delight of K.C. with his new toys, the memories of a wonderful Christmas Eve dinner in our own home, the midnight service in church, the late-night Bill-and-Pann dishwashing session—all these are full of life and joy that will always warm our hearts. And as of today I can also say that God has used not only me, but Bill and K.C. as well, each day in spite of my illness. So my daily request is the same: "Lord, make each day count for quality living and giving, and use me in spite of illness, tiredness, or a foreboding future. Amen."

Pann read the pages she had written two days before in her journal, noting the date March 14, 1976. It didn't seem possible that she had spent a whole year battling this affliction. Yet in a very real sense, the year had held a lot of good. Never before had she felt the unwavering spotlight of God's power and love zeroed in on her with such unblinking intensity, nor had the truth of God's Word ever been so self-evident. "Now unto Him Who is able . . ." How often had she heard those words at the end of a church service but failed to embrace them in her heart. *How sad that people have to be pushed to their limits before they discover the power of that simple statement, "He is able,"* Pann thought as she turned to a clean page and began to write: "Of all God's special gifts to me in this year of illness, K.C. has been the most precious. For both Bill and me, the unqualified enthusiasm he has had for life and the sparkling sweetness of his laughing smile have lifted our burdens and our spirits."

Pann paused, visualizing K.C.'s tousled blond curls and big blue eyes. Oh, how she hated being away from him! Tonight Bill would bring him for a visit. Her arms ached to hold him, even though he was no longer an infant. Those days were long gone, and she had missed most of them. Already he had changed from a baby to an active toddler.

> With each of my strokes, he has given me a special reason to get well. Unlike Bill, who loves me so deeply that he would care for me no matter how weak I stayed, K.C. needs me to be just as healthy and mobile as I can possibly be. So on those days when the therapy has been discouraging, the desire to be the best possible mother I can be to my special son has given me the courage to keep trying.
>
> There is an irony, however, to my statements about K.C.'s lifting our burdens. Without K.C. to worry about, the responsibility weighing on Bill, the need for my mother's and friends' help, the worry in my own mind would have been far less. But no gift is without a price. Our salvation through Christ is a free gift, but it was not made available to us without the price of pain and death paid by our Lord at Calvary. Thus the gift of K.C.'s love, life, and joy to us has had the ironic characteristic of creating a burden of concern for this little fellow we love so much, while easing an even greater burden of sorrow and despair.
>
> I should also mention that K.C. has been a gift to others as well. He has been a special source of love and laughter to my mother and our friends, and has brought the priceless gift of a cheerier day to countless patients and staff members.
>
> Lord Jesus, thank You for K.C. Thank You for the burden and the blessing he has brought into our lives. We're richer for his life. Thank You for the courage that his needing me has given me.

The last words were written through a blur of tears. Pann dated the page and put the notebook away. These days, the thought of how much she loved K.C. and Bill always brought tears to her eyes. "Silly woman," she mumbled as she impatiently dabbed her eyes and gave her nose a blow. Then she ran a comb through her hair and smoothed her bed covers in preparation for a visit from her two men. It had been several days since K.C.'s last visit, and after writing about him, Pann was bursting with impatience to see him.

"Hi, Honey," Bill greeted Pann as he walked into the room with an apologetic air. "No, I didn't bring K.C.," he added quickly, as Pann's look of anticipation turned into a question. "He's still got a cough, and your mother felt he shouldn't be out in the night air. With his eye operation in a couple of weeks, we don't want him to get sick or run-down. I'll bring him tomorrow if he's better. Besides, won't I do?" Bill asked, bending to give Pann a kiss.

"Yes, of course," Pann answered with a smile that did little to hide her disappointment. "It's just that I really needed to see him tonight. You know how I hate the idea of his having this operation while I'm still in the hospital."

"Now, Pann, we have talked this all out. We agreed that the operation shouldn't wait. And it's a perfect time, with your mother already here to take care of him. Even if you were home, you couldn't take care of him. This way, by the time you come home, K.C. will be all better and hopefully we'll be through with hospitals for a while."

"Forever would be fine with me," Pann sighed.

"Me, too," Bill agreed as he pulled a chair over to Pann's bed. "But for you to be truly well, we've got to find some answers, and I'm beginning to seriously doubt that we're asking the right people to do the finding. Now I've been thinking and—"

"Bill, I really don't want to talk about this right now." Pann interrupted in an attempt to avoid the confrontation that had been building ever since her close brush with death. "I'm telling you that the *last* thing I need to do is change doctors. These men know me. They've been with me from the beginning."

"And I'm telling *you* that there's something wrong here. You almost died from the Dilantin, and that's not the first mistake that's been made! Your parents, your cousins, Phyllis, my folks—we all agree that there must be something they are overlooking. There must be!" Bill rose from his chair and strode angrily over to the window. *Why was Pann defending these men? Surely she knew that all he wanted was to find someone who could help her.* "This just can't go on and on," he said more calmly, studying the tree-lined street below. "We need some answers, and if these men can't find them, then maybe we should find someone who can."

Pann looked at her husband's dejected face and realized once more how hard the past year had been on him. It wasn't difficult to understand his frustration. She shared it. But somehow she had to make him understand her need to believe in the men who literally held her life in their hands. If she allowed herself to join Bill and her family in criticizing and placing blame, she would destroy the one stabilizing factor in her chaotic life—her trust in her doctors' ability to make her well.

Pann believed in God's sovereign rule over life and death and in His power to heal. But the past year had taught her that the miracle of healing is not always instantaneous. It can come more slowly through natural processes aided by the skill and knowledge of medical science. She saw her doctors and nurses as God's instruments of healing, and her trust in them was a lifeline feeding her soul the way an IV fed her body. It was essential to her emotional survival.

"Bill, please try to understand," Pann pleaded, trying to breach the wall that separated them. "Doctor Martin and Doctor Eisenberg are good men. Yes, I had an allergic reaction to the Dilantin. But no one could have foreseen that, and if they hadn't responded as quickly as they did, I would have died! I owe them my life! I trust them. I need them! Doctor Martin treats me like his own daughter. He really cares about me, and I won't suddenly turn away from him in favor of some stranger!"

"I see. Afraid you won't have your boyfriend there to hold your hand?" The words were out of Bill's mouth before he could stop them. He himself was shocked by the bitterness of his tone. He turned to look at Pann, an apology on his lips, but the cold expression on her face froze the words in his throat.

Later that night at the Kilian's, Bill recounted, "I can't help it. Sometimes I'm so jealous of Pann's dependence on her doctors, I feel like the Jolly Green Giant. I know it's stupid. They're her doctors. She's supposed to listen to them and depend on them. But there just isn't any question who's more important in her life these days. I'm just the guy who brings her peanuts and magazines. *They* are the ones who keep her alive."

Paul rapidly countered, "And just where do you think Pann would be without peanuts and magazines? Not to mention the insurance you work so hard to provide, which pays the bills, and all the love, encouragement, and prayers you represent. If Pann didn't have you and K.C. to come home to, do you honestly believe all the doctors in the world could give her the desire to keep going? She *needs* them to get well, but *you* are the ones she is getting well for. Right?" Paul asked with an encouraging nod.

"Yeah, I guess so, although sometimes I even wonder about that," Bill said.

"What do you mean?"

"In the beginning I knew Pann really looked forward to

99

seeing me. My visits meant something. She'd perk up when I entered the room, and we'd talk—you know—*really* talk. But lately I just don't seem to matter that much. It's all for K.C. If I go by myself it's just old Bill—nothing special. Half the time we just sit there and watch television, barely talking. But if I bring K.C. with me, she lights up like a Christmas tree. Her voice comes alive and she's her old self, full of laughter and spirit. I'd give anything to see her light up like that for me."

"You know, Bill," Paul replied, "I can remember a time, not long after Gloria and I had our first child, when I felt the same way about us. I was so jealous of that baby! Not that I ever would have put it that way. To a certain degree, it's hard for any man to adjust to the fact that the woman who was once first and foremost his wife and lover is now a mother—with all those famous instincts we're always hearing about. Of course Pann looks forward to seeing K.C. Being separated from him at his young age has got to be torment for her. But that doesn't mean she loves you any less. She just doesn't feel the need to give to you like she gives to him."

That night and throughout the next day Bill mulled over Paul's words. His head knew that Paul was right, but his heart needed time to heal. He didn't visit Pann for a couple of days, and when he did, he felt nervous and unsure of what to say. He and Pann didn't fight often. They were both uncomfortable with confrontation and tended to internalize their emotions rather than risk an argument.

Now Bill hesitated outside Pann's door to take a few deep breaths before entering. The sound of a deep, rattling cough made him forget the clever opening line he'd rehearsed all the way to the hospital. He pushed the door open and walked into the room. "Mouse, you all right? Where'd that cough come from?"

Pann looked up with undisguised joy and relief. Three days

was a long time for Bill to stay away. While the "boyfriend" remark had stung her deeply, her anger had faded when she realized how much she missed him. "Beats me. I was lying here minding my own business and it just started up. It's probably an infection from being on the respirator, but they're giving me something for it, so don't worry." Pann took a breath and reached out a hand. "It's sure good to see you. I missed you."

"Me, too," Bill said, sitting by her side on the bed. "I love you, Pann Baltz. I may not always know how to say it, but you mean everything to me. All I want is for you to get well."

"I know that. And I love you too. It's just that sometimes I feel so far away from you and K.C. It's like I've been exiled to · another world, totally cut off from what once was normal and real, and I get scared that I'm not going to make it back again. My whole life is this hospital. I don't have anything else to talk about, and at times I just don't know what to say to you. I've lost touch, and I don't know how to reconnect!"

Bill held Pann for a long time before they started talking again and they didn't stop until the night nurse came in to tell them that visiting hours were over. The next night Bill arrived with K.C. in one arm and some magazines and dry-roasted peanuts in the other. He watched with joy as the little boy wriggled out of his grasp and ran into his mother's open arms. Later, as Bill wearily slipped off his coat and sat down on the edge of his bed, he found this note tucked in his coat pocket.

Hi, Sweetie,
I feel the need to communicate with you, to be able to write down something so special for you to have today to read when you are alone. I want to be able to say something unique and new, and yet what comes to me in the stillness of this time is just the deep awareness of how much you are with me at all times. It is the quiet reassurance that I am deeply loved by you. It is that love which in great measure

has carried me through these rough days and will continue to sustain in me the knowledge that I am disabled in body *only*. Thank you for letting me share with you in all of life. . . . It's exciting to greet each day with the feeling of being loved and joined to you.

I love you.

It was signed with the sketch of a happy little mouse.

Above: Richard, Eileen, Dick, Pann Langford, 1964. *Right:* Pann as a Hollywood High cheerleader, 1967.

Pann and Bill's wedding, 1969.

Left: Pann and K.C. after the second stroke. *Above left:* Pann tried hard to keep her sense of humor during isolation. *Above:* Pann, K.C., and their neighbor, Marie, trick-or-treating in IMCU, 1976.

K.C. with Phyllis's daughters while Pann was in Denver.

Right: Pann, Bill, and K.C. a few days before open heart, 1979. *Below:* Pann and Lois Bach after platelet donation.

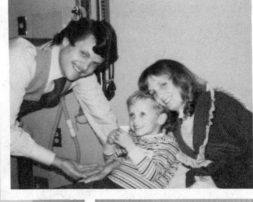

Above: Cartoon for Dr. Matloff: "Jack be nimble, Jack be quick. Make my heart to tick, tick, tick!" *Left:* Gloria Killian (l.), Pann, and Darlene and Kernie Kostub (r.)— K.C.'s other families.

Left: Eileen Langford with K.C., age four. *Below:* Bill and Dr. Herb Downie.

The Baltz family, 1987.

XIV

A S WITH MANY of Pann's problems, her "little cough" didn't go away. Within a week it had developed into a raging staph infection in her lungs, and she found herself in isolation for two weeks. No one was allowed in her room without wearing a gown, mask, and gloves, and her world was reduced to four bare walls, disposable dishes, and silence. More than anything, the lack of human contact got to Pann. She had fought long and hard to stay on top of her illness. She had refused to give in to despair and defeat. But she needed the stimulation of conversation and life going on around her to distract her from the negative thoughts that constantly lurked in the shadows of her mind. Now she felt like a pile of flesh and bones, racked with fever and dazed by frequent codeine injections—an untouchable, alone with her fears and depression.

Characteristically, Pann didn't give in without a fight. After her first week in isolation, Bill arrived to find a large sign decorated with colorful flowers taped to Pann's door. In large, bright letters it read, "Pann Baltz, Chief of Staph." Still, the isolation drained her of more than physical strength.

Shortly after her release from isolation, Dr. Martin decided to send Pann home. She still had a troublesome cough that required codeine several times a day, but he felt that after four months in the hospital, home would be the best medicine. So they taught Pann how to give herself the injections and sent her home with a generous supply of medication.

Home! Pann stood for several seconds in the entryway, looking around—feeling, smelling, waiting for the overwhelming sense of relief to hit her. But as she made her way into the living room and sank down on the couch, she couldn't shake a feeling of unreality. She had been gone too long and been through too much to return as though she'd never been away. The next few days were a time of transition from patient to person. After four months in a bed or wheelchair, just walking from room to room was a challenge, and it took Pann days to get over the sensation that the floors were uneven.

Pann also felt off balance in her relationship with Bill. Once again she had to deal with insecurities about her attractiveness, while Bill found himself torn between the desire to reassure and comfort her and his own natural impatience to have his wife back. Both felt unsure of themselves and afraid of rejection; neither knew how to communicate their feelings in an open, healthy way. That week was full of awkward moments as both of them fumbled their way back toward oneness.

Only Pann's relationship with K.C. seemed to have gone unscathed. Marveling at how much he'd changed, she couldn't take her eyes off him. He'd learned new words, new skills, and many other things she hadn't been able to appreciate during his hospital visits. It also became clear that she and Bill had made the right decision in asking their friend Melody to stay with them for a while. It would be some time before Pann could take care of her active eighteen-month-old by herself.

Eventually life fell into a routine. Pann received outpatient therapy three times a week, and her progress was encouraging. But while her physical recovery was good, her emotional life entered an increasingly difficult and complex phase. As a young girl, Pann had been taught the fundamentals of faith, being rooted in God's Word. Until now that foundation had held her steady, kicking in like an automatic pilot when her own strength failed. But Pann's ordeal had lasted over a year, and while her spirit was strong, her body and soul were exhausted.

Pann: "When I came home from the hospital, my face and speech were back to normal, my right arm was about eighty percent there, and I could walk with the help of a brace and a cane. But I don't honestly believe that *inside* I was anywhere close to being healed. 'Shattered' would be a good way to describe my emotions. And the worst part was that I couldn't admit it. When I went to church or when people would call, I'd just go on about how good God had been to bring me through this experience. I'd talk about how He was sustaining me and was always with me. And looking back from where I am today, I know that all I said was true! But at the time I'm not sure I really believed it. I was *so* petrified, after all that I had been through in just one year's time, that everything was colored by the fear of what might come next!

"I truly believe I could have saved myself a lot of pain and even physical complications if I had believed that God loved me enough to hear my anger. If there is one thing I want other people to learn from my mistakes it is that God is big enough to handle our anger and hurt! He's not going to reject or punish us for being honest about our feelings. After all, He created every human emotion. He understands that anger and fear must be expressed in a healthy way, to keep them from festering inside and poisoning our whole being. If only I could have cried out my fears and cleansed my soul of all that negative thought and energy! But instead I kept pushing it down, denying it, and keeping up the victorious front that I thought everyone expected of me and would approve of."

This inner turmoil left Pann vulnerable to the seductive side effects of her medication. Although the doctor's prescription contained only a mild narcotic, it offered Pann an emotional escape that lifted her above her anxieties into a gentle, sleepy haze. Soon she was taking the drug to relieve the pain in her heart as much as to control the cough in her lungs. The medication numbed her emotions but had little effect on the infection. By the middle of June she was back in the hospital for serious respiratory treatment.

It was Friday. Pann had been in the hospital about a week for respiratory therapy that had done little to alleviate her problem. In fact, she had had severe chest pains a few days before and had been given increasing amounts of narcotic to ease her discomfort. The result was a perpetual fog that enshrouded her senses and robbed her of any keen awareness of time or place. Yet even the drugs couldn't dull the panic Pann felt as she listened to her own wheezing gasps for breath and heard the doctor confirm that she was going into stridor.

Blood gases were immediately taken. The results were bad: She didn't have enough oxygen in her bloodstream. The call went out for Dr. Eisenberg.

"Call Bill. Please. Somebody call my husband," Pann cried out into the general hubbub as she was once again raced to ICU.

Bill raced to the hospital in record time and pushed his way into the ICU to catch a glimpse of Pann and let her know he was there. An ashen face and heaving chest was all he saw before a white-coated young man took him firmly by the arm and pushed him back toward the door. "Sorry, Sir. You'll have to wait outside."

"But my wife! How's my wife?" Bill demanded.

"I'm sure she'll be fine if you'll let us do our job. Please! Wait outside!"

Bill backed reluctantly toward the door, his eyes searching the room for a familiar face. "Where's the anesthesiologist?" Dr. Eisenberg's voice rang out over the organized confusion. "Why isn't he here?"

Bill felt a physical rush of relief at the sight of the homely, familiar face. But his relief was short-lived.

"He's unavailable. On another case," someone replied.

"Well, we can't wait or we'll lose her. We'll have to go ahead without him." Dr. Eisenberg's words were the last Bill heard as the door was firmly shut behind him, and the shades were pulled down to cover the windows of the glass cubicle.

Shaking and stunned, Bill stood uncertainly outside the door, trying to decide what to do. His helplessness filled him with a paralyzing rage. He sat on a bench against the wall while the seconds ticked by in silence.

The scream came out of nowhere, a high, screeching wail of agony, more animal than human, shattering the quiet like a shotgun blast through a window. *Pann?* Bill froze on the bench, his breath locked within his chest. Another scream, not as surprised as the first, more rooted in pain.

Bill jumped to his feet, ready to break through the door until his attention was drawn to the bottom of the glass wall. The shades didn't quite reach the floor, leaving about a foot of uncovered glass, through which Bill could see feet dashing from one place to the other. Or more specifically, shoes—shoes covered with green booties now splattered with red, the same red that dotted the floor and speckled the bottom of the windows. Blood—Pann's blood.

The screams were now moans, constant, pathetic, pleading.

"No! No! No!" Bill rasped through gritted teeth. "I can't take any more. Do you hear, God? No more!" He buried his face in his hands and rocked unsteadily back and forth on the balls of his feet. The urge to run was overpowering. "I'll go home, pack a bag, get K.C., get out. I have to get out!" Without conscious thought, Bill found himself escaping down the hall toward the elevator, pushing the button, watching the doors close behind him. Safe inside the elevator, he stood staring at the panel of buttons. *Which one to push? Where to go?* The questions overwhelmed him. He stood frozen for several moments, unwilling to think and afraid to feel. Finally he reached toward the panel and pushed "Door Open."

The walk back to the ICU was not an easy one. Bill felt incredibly old and bone-tired. He hated what he knew awaited him in that little room—the nightmare of Pann's pain. The disappointment and frustration of more problems and no answers. The constant fear of losing the woman he loved, coupled with the fear of being trapped in this hellish situation. Yet he had no choice. That was *Pann* in that room, not some stranger. Pann, the one who wrote him funny notes and never failed to laugh at his corny jokes (well, almost never). Pann, the mother of his child. Pann, his lover and his friend. As Bill would say years later, "A man might consider walking out on his wife when times get really tough. It happens every day in our so-called sophisticated society. But you don't walk away from your best friend."

The doctors saved Pann's life once again, and Bill stayed by her side through the night. To keep her from choking, he learned how to suction the blood that oozed around the breathing tube in her mouth. Once during those long, dark hours he nearly lost her when her heart went into fibrillation; it wasn't until early morning that her blood gases began to register an increased level of oxygen, an encouraging sign of improvement. Amazingly, Pann had improved enough by Sunday to have the respiratory tube removed and seemed to be on her way to recovery. They had both made it through one more crisis.

Two weeks later Pann's breathing shut off again. It happened very suddenly and for no apparent reason. They immediately began to prepare her to go back on the respirator, and the very thought of it threw Pann into a frenzy. Desperately searching the crowded room, she signaled to a young nurse she knew was a Christian. She knew she was putting her friend on the spot in front of all the other staff in the room, but there was no time to be subtle. Grabbing the nurse's hand, Pann gasped, "I don't think I can go through this again! Please help me. Pray with me!"

The young woman only hesitated an instant before bowing her head and praying in a full voice that belied any self-consciousness she might have felt. She prayed for God's peace to fill Pann's heart and mind and for the procedure to be done smoothly and without pain.

Minutes later Pann was informed that because of her heart, she could not be put to sleep as she had begged, though the anesthesiologist promised to do everything he could to spare her unnecessary discomfort. His reassurances meant little to Pann, who watched with growing panic as they prepared to insert the tube. *Oh, God, just strike me dead. Let me die before the pain,* she pleaded silently, closing her eyes and stiffening in anticipation of the worst. But the pain never came. She felt only a slight discomfort as the tube slid down her throat, and once she felt the blessed relief of clear, fresh oxygen filling her lungs, she knew the worst was over. Tears of relief spilled down her face, and Pann praised God for honoring a nurse's courageous prayer of faith.

XV

Lungs can actually forget how to breathe, which is why doctors try to wean their patients off the respirator as soon as possible. When Pann was still unable to breathe on her own after a week, an ear-nose-and-throat specialist was called in. Pann's vocal cords, he discovered, were paralyzed. As he explained to Bill and Pann, vocal cords have two functions: to vibrate as we exhale, producing our voice; and to separate when we inhale, allowing air into the air passage leading to the lungs. In Pann's case, the cords refused to part when she inhaled, thereby blocking the intake of air. Just why the cords were paralyzed or for how long, the doctor didn't know.

The doctors decided to make an incision in Pann's throat and insert a trach tube, which would bypass the uncooperative cords and allow air to pass directly into her air passage. While the tracheotomy made breathing easier and was comparatively painless, it took Pann nearly a week to summon the courage to examine her neck in a mirror. The trach was made out of white tubing and stuck out about an inch, making it almost impossible to cover.

"I look like the bride of Frankenstein!" she wrote to Bill in exasperation, unable to speak because the trach had not yet been fitted with a flap that would allow her to talk.

"Naw, she was taller," Bill teased with a straight face. Pann's shoulders shook with silent laughter. It felt good. It seemed like ages since she'd laughed or even smiled. The past few weeks had passed in a blur of pain and depression. Even her sleep was unnatural and polluted by unpleasant dreams, offering no real escape or refreshment.

Pann watched as Bill continued to talk. She saw his mouth move and his hands gesture, but somehow the effort of concentrating on what he was saying was too much. She was totally exhausted. Somewhere locked deep inside was Pann Baltz—pretty, smart, talented, and funny—the girl everyone liked and admired for her courage and strength of character. But that Pann was lost in a maze of pain and codeine; what was left was eighty pounds of anger, fear, and frustration.

Since she didn't know how to release the mounting volcano of emotions within her, Pann's anger spilled out onto those around her. She became difficult and demanding. For the first time in her life, she knew what it was to be disliked by her nurses.

Deciding they could do no more for her in the hospital, the doctors sent Pann home with her trach in place, plugged so that she could talk in a thin, breathy voice. She was also given a fresh supply of needles and codeine, since she still suffered with the painful staph infection in her chest. She was to continue physical therapy three times a week and see the ENT specialist as an outpatient.

But going home was not the joy and relief it had once been.

Pann was physically depleted and emotionally whipped. She hated the way she looked with the tube in her neck. She felt guilty about the burden she had dumped on Bill, and she ached that her son didn't have a strong, healthy mother to take care of him. Watching Melody clean her house and do the hundred and one other things that were Pann's right and responsibility as a wife and mother filled Pann with a sense of uselessness. She despaired that she would ever be normal again. Her first appointment with the ENT specialist was the bitter icing on the cake.

"The bottom line is that I can't find any physical reason for your inability to breathe," the doctor said with a brisk, no-nonsense air. "My suggestion is that you see a good psychiatrist. It's my bet that after a couple of appointments I'll be able to take your trach out."

Horrified, Pann listened as the man behind the desk casually shrugged off her problem as emotional, or "functional," as the medical profession terms it. Was it her imagination or did she hear a note of disdain in his voice? Was his look really a little colder, slightly accusing? When he said "functional," why did she hear "intentional"? Pann had heard about this feeling from other patients labeled functional. There was a subtle change in the attitude of the staff, a posture that said, "Sorry you're sick, but you *are* doing it to yourself."

When Pann told Dr. Eisenberg about the specialist's conclusion, he was adamant in his reassurance that the man was wrong. "Vocal cords are not voluntary muscles and cannot be controlled by emotions, conscious or unconscious," he insisted, angry that Pann was being dealt one more unnecessary blow. Even if her problem were functional, he explained, a functional illness is produced by emotions buried deep within the subconscious, totally beyond the control of the will. And the symptoms are every bit as real as those from physical illness and just as serious.

Pann had accepted long ago that a certain percentage of her problem was bound to be functionally based. Everyone who experiences a long traumatic illness is going to suffer some emotional backlash. But the idea that she had unconsciously willed herself to stop breathing and was responsible for the hideous tube in her neck—not to mention all the pain she'd endured and the hell Bill had gone through—was almost more than she could stand.

Traditionally, summer is a time for trips to the beach and lazy days lying in the sun, soaking up rays. But the long hot days offered Pann little respite as she continued therapy and struggled to regain some sense of independence. Her recovery was slow but steady. By the end of the summer she was able to handle K.C. and the household chores pretty much on her own. She felt great relief when the doctors removed her trach in late August. Still, the chest pains continued, and so did her depression, which drove her into dark spells of hopelessness and self-pity that only the codeine seemed to lift. By this time she was injecting herself every two or three hours, just to stay on the top of the pain.

During this time, Pann's folks came to visit. They found their daughter drastically changed. She was distant, hard to reach, distracted by the drugs, and increasingly defensive as she sought to protect herself from a world that seemed suddenly alien and hostile. She began to secretly see herself as a horrible person upon whom the wrath of God had descended. Nothing her parents did seemed to help. None of the old formulas were working. Her life was riddled with questions, not just about her physical illness, but about her own value as a person. She was desperate for answers. Finally Pann's father decided to inter-vene.

Dick Langford: "When Pann's strokes continued and some of her doctors began to say her problem was functional, I decided that she must have help from a good psychiatrist. I did not agree with those doctors, and I struggled over making the suggestion that she see someone, because I didn't want her to think that I did. But I saw in my daughter a great sense of fear and perplexity, and I wanted her to have her doubts alleviated.

"The best psychiatrist I knew was Dr. Ron Griffith, and I recall sitting in Pann's kitchen, talking to her about seeing him. She agreed with such ease and eagerness that I was surprised. I called Ron and made her first appointment."

Up until this time, Pann had strongly resisted the idea of seeing a psychiatrist. The very idea suggested a lack of inner strength and stability that she found both offensive and terrifying. Besides, good Christians weren't supposed to need that kind of worldly counsel. What would her friends think if they knew she was going to a "shrink"? Worst of all, wouldn't seeing a psychiatrist be, in effect, an admission that there was really something mentally wrong with her?

But as her father spoke that day, Pann realized that Dr. Griffith couldn't possibly make her feel any worse than she already did, and he just might help. At least she'd give it a try.

Pann's first appointment was the first week of September. Dr. Griffith proved to be an excellent counselor, with a special ability to incorporate sound biblical principles into an expert psychiatric practice. As is usually the case, during the first few sessions Pann did most of the talking.

Pann: "I remember describing myself as 'fiercely independent.' I now know that when someone overemphasizes a point, they often do so because they don't feel very secure in that area. The truth probably was that I was a very dependent person. My illness was making me more aware of my dependency, and I was scared to death!"

The opportunity to finally express her innermost feelings to someone who would neither judge nor condemn was like throwing open the windows of her soul and allowing a cool, fresh breeze to clear away the smoke that had been choking the life out of her. While they had only taken the first small steps down what would prove to be a long and difficult path, on the surface Pann appeared to make almost immediate progress. The weight of depression that had pinned her down for so long began to lift, and traces of the old Pann began to resurface.

Most importantly, Pann found the courage to look honestly at her circumstances and to evaluate not only what her illness had meant in the past, but how it would affect the rest of her life. After the first stroke, there had been no reason to expect that she would not fully recover. But now, after all that had happened during the past year, she accepted the fact that she might never be one hundred percent physically well again. Facing up to this truth was painful but strangely releasing. She wrote to her parents:

> For a long time, probably since I broke my foot [before K.C. was born], I have been waiting for our life to be "normal" again. The truth that God has finally revealed to me is that what is normal for another family may not be normal for us. I can no longer wait for life to be normal or meaningful only after I stop being sick, for I now know that I have a disease that is going to mean hospital trips for me each year for some time to come. This is our "norm," and we must accept it and make our lives as meaningful as we can within that scope and pattern. It is not a giving up of hope that I'll ever get well, but rather looking at life realistically.

I believe a great part of this summer's depression was due to the medication I was on, as well as my understandable frustration. I was recently reminded of Lloyd Ogilvie's definition of depression. He said that the depth of our depression is in direct proportion to the difference between what we thought and what truly is. For you, Mother, that probably explains the depth of your hurt for me, in that my life pattern now is far different than what you'd imagined it would be (healthy, active, etc.). It also explains mine this summer—the difference between what I'd thought would be happening (full independence and mobility) as measured against what I really had (critical illness and total dependence).

I have accepted now that there will be periodic setbacks and the need for help with K.C. But I also believe I have a better chance of improving as the years go by. That hope is what I have now. As for the rest of it, I'm napping lots, talking normally, and feeling good. I am truly better.

XVI

I T WAS A SUNDAY EVENING in mid-October. Bill arched his back and tried to stretch his long legs as he drove the last few miles home from the lake. At first he had resisted the idea of leaving Pann alone for the weekend. But she was feeling so much better that she had convinced him she would be fine for a couple of days without him. He had left the Friday before, feeling as giddy as a boy off on a great adventure.

For two glorious days he had indulged himself in his favorite pastime: rising early in the brisk mountain air to take a boat out on the glassy waters and fish to his heart's content. It had been ages since he had done something just for the pure, selfish pleasure of it, and he desperately needed the break. For the past year and a half, the pressure had been unrelenting— not only Pann's situation, but his work as well. Bill usually tried not to make a big deal out of his work problems, feeling that Pann was already carrying as much of a burden as she could bear.

But that didn't mean problems didn't arise. In a large and competitive company like Xerox, it was inevitable that he would be confronted with personality conflicts or difficult situations, not to mention the constant demands to produce and stay on top.

Lately it seemed Bill was knocking heads with his new boss over every little thing. The man obviously didn't like him and let him know it. With his past track record, Bill wasn't worried about losing his job, but the daily friction was wearing, and he hated being constantly on the defensive.

Bill: "It's a shame that the problems at work came right when I desperately needed someone to build me up. Most people get the positive reinforcement they need from their mates, but much of the time during those years Pann couldn't be there for me, so I looked for it at work. If I had been made to feel my own worth and value as a human being, instead of being constantly belittled, it would have made all the difference. I desperately needed to be touched on a personal level, to have someone sit me down and say, 'I know you're hurting and worried much of the time, but that's okay. You are still doing a good job, and I appreciate the extra effort it takes.' Unfortunately no one ever said anything like that, and I just had to weather it through. But I learned a valuable lesson about the fragility of the human spirit, and I hope I deal with those under me with greater sensitivity and understanding because of it."

Keeping his personal life from affecting his work was a constant struggle. People at work knew about Pann's condition, and a day didn't go by without Bill hearing the obligatory "How's Pann?" Knowing they didn't really want a full report, he usually resorted to one or two standard replies. What bothered him, however, was that people rarely expressed a sincere interest in how *he* was doing. The only person at work who showed personal concern for him was a young woman who entered his office one day to explain that she understood how difficult it must be for him with Pann in the hospital all the time and to offer her "condolences" whenever he felt inclined. Loosening his tie in the suddenly stuffy room, Bill politely but firmly declined her offer. As she walked out the door he thought, *Now, that kind of concern I don't need!*

That weekend, the lazy, undisturbed hours on the lake gave Bill time to examine his deeper feelings. He'd had months to resign himself to the supporting role of "Pann's husband," but it was still a part for which he felt poorly cast. Even at church, people seemed oddly insensitive to Bill's emotional needs. A few people—Paul Kilian and several of the pastors—had shown concern for Bill's welfare, but for the most part, Pann's life-or-death circumstances eclipsed Bill's less dramatic suffering.

In the boat that weekend, Bill listened to the gentle waves lapping against the side and stared out at the endless expanse of blue sky. He felt at peace. The warm autumn sun melted away layer after layer of tension and self-pity, and his spirits began to rise as he meditated on the things for which he could be grateful. After all, Pann was better, and life was starting to feel normal again. K.C. was fine. His eyes had healed well after his corrective surgery, and he and Bill enjoyed a close and loving relationship, one of the few benefits of Pann's hospitalizations. The truly important thing was that the three of them were together again. Bill felt a quiet optimism stirring in his soul.

Driving home on Sunday, he felt more refreshed than he had in months. Although he had enjoyed every minute of his time away, he was anxious to get home and see Pann and K.C.

As Bill pulled into the driveway, immediately he knew that something was wrong. The house was dark—no porch light, no lights in any windows. He unlocked the front door, and his worried "hello" echoed through the empty house. With his heart in his throat, he walked woodenly to the phone and dialed the hospital. Pann was in intensive care. She had suffered another stroke.

Bill raced to the hospital. Hurrying down the now familiar hallways, he tried to prepare himself for what he might find. After all, they'd been through this before; he knew what to expect. Still, beads of nervous perspiration gathered on his forehead, and he could taste the familiar bile of dread as he entered the ICU ward and greeted Dr. Martin.

"How is she, Doc?" he asked without preliminaries.

"I'm not really sure," the doctor answered honestly. "She was admitted about four hours ago, obviously in the midst of another stroke. Then about an hour ago she seemed to have a seizure, and she hasn't regained consciousness since. I don't think she's in any immediate danger, but we'll just have to watch her closely and see what happens."

After a few minutes of holding Pann's unresponsive hand and reassuring her that she was going to be all right, Bill walked wearily to the pay phone and placed a call to Seattle. Oh, how he hated making that call! Why did he always have to be the one to give the bad news? *Pann's parents must dread the very sound of my voice,* he thought, feeling his eyes burn and his throat constrict as the connection was made and the phone began to ring.

"Hello, Mom? It's Bill. I'm afraid I've got bad news."

XVII

PANN: "I didn't regain consciousness until the next day, when it was explained to me that I'd suffered a grand-mal seizure. The doctors weren't sure what had caused it, but they didn't seem overly concerned until later that day, when I had another one and then another. That began a period of extensive testing to find the right medication to control the seizures.

"I could always tell when a seizure was coming on. First I'd feel the pressure building in my head and funny lights would dance before my eyes. Then my body would begin to jerk, and I'd lose control of my bowels and bladder. The uncontrolled shaking would cause me to bite my tongue and lips, and I would usually wake up with a bloody mouth.

"I also suffered with terrible pain in my head, and it was a standing order that I could ask for a hundred milligrams of Demerol every three hours if I needed it—a privilege I rarely failed to exercise. This is a horrible time for me to look back on.

My memory is jumbled and hazy. Mother and Bill remember better than I."

Eileen Langford: "The period of the seizures was the most horrible time of the whole experience. Sometimes Pann would have ten or eleven within an hour's time. Her little body would practically break in two, and nothing could be done. I knew in my heart that she was dying, but nobody would say so. Her doctor was upset with us for even suggesting she was that critical. He kept insisting the seizures wouldn't hurt her. Later I learned they can be very damaging.

"Pann would get a wild-eyed expression on her face. She knew something terrible was happening. She was a virtual prisoner in that body. She lost weight, and I could barely stand to look at her. She was dying before our eyes, and there was nothing anyone could do.

"We were at the hospital day and night. Bill's mother, Ruth, and I took the night shifts so Bill could sleep. I would watch the baby during the day, then sleep until midnight, and then relieve Ruth. They didn't have enough hospital staff and someone had to watch Pann every minute to call for help when she had a seizure. There was no one else in her room, so we could lay down for brief naps if we needed to. Mostly I just sat and watched her. After Christmas her father came down from Seattle and took over the all-night shift."

Bill: "I don't remember how I lived through the seizures. I was just so desperate to help Pann. I'd seen her have seizures, and she'd just shake. No control. No warning. They tied her in bed so she wouldn't fall out, but she still got bruised. Her mouth was all chewed up and she was in constant pain. I remember sitting by her side in a darkened room and listening to her sob and ask over and over, 'Why?' Never before had I felt so helpless. There just weren't any answers. The only thing I could think to say was that maybe Pann was called to be a martyr."

Pann: "A specialist from USC was called in. He thought that I might be having heart rhythms that were depriving my brain of oxygen and causing my seizures. Another theory was that I had epilepsy, but I never believed it. My EEG wasn't normal because of my strokes, but I did not have a focal seizure point. With epilepsy you can find something on the EEG to pinpoint seizure activity, but they never could with me.

"The result of all the uncertainty was more and more medication. Still I had seizures every day, anywhere, whether I was in my room or in a testing room; in bed or on a gurney. It didn't matter. Between the seizure medication and the Demerol, I was so drugged that I think I went a little crazy. I don't even remember who took care of K.C. during that time. I do remember that we celebrated his second birthday in my room at the hospital. I was strapped in bed with padding all around it, looking drawn and awful. I couldn't even hold him.

"Sometime early in December the doctors recognized that I was addicted to the Demerol and had to be taken off it. I was a hospital junkie, addicted by prescription and as totally hooked as an addict on the street.

"The physical part of my withdrawal was extremely unpleasant. I felt very sick for a few days with nausea, chills, sweats, and cramps. But it was the emotional dependency that was agonizing. Getting the narcotic became the most important thing in my life, and I became angry and abusive when people wouldn't give it to me. I pleaded. I begged. I demanded. I even went through a period of making telephone calls to anyone I thought might possibly help. One day I called my father in Seattle and frightened him so much with my hysterics that he called my doctor demanding to know what was going on."

Bill: "I think I came closest to throwing up my hands and walking away during Pann's phone-call period. She would call me at night pleading for help. I knew she was incoherent. There was nothing I could do. Sometimes I'd go over and sit with her. But most nights I'd just listen and try to calm her on the phone. There were nights when she would call three or four times and I would be tempted to take the phone off the hook just to get a few hours of uninterrupted sleep. But I was too afraid that something would happen and the doctors wouldn't be able to reach me, so I never did.

"Unfortunately I wasn't the only one Pann pestered. In her depression she called every doctor she had ever seen or heard of. She even tried to get in touch with Jerry Calloway, which wouldn't have been surprising, except he was in Korea at the time. Finally, in self-defense, her doctors ordered her phone disconnected, but I put my foot down, insisting she be allowed to call me. After that, all her calls were monitored.

"One night she called and asked me to bring what was left of her home supply of codeine to the hospital, so she could personally give it to Dr. Martin in the morning. I thought making the gesture might help her psychologically, so I agreed. The night nurse wanted me to give the drugs to her when I arrived, but I explained the situation and promised to sit with Pann all night to make sure there was no problem. I put the package in the closet and settled in a chair for the night.

"Later Pann awoke, calling for a bedpan. She asked me to step out and give her some privacy. The nurse immediately suggested she remove the codeine, but I said no. I sat outside Pann's door and waited. Suddenly there was a crash from within. Somehow Pann had used the bedpan to loosen her straps and had fallen trying to get up.

"'I heard K.C. crying,' she claimed with tears in her eyes. 'I just wanted to help him.'

"'K.C. crying, indeed,' the nurse sniffed coldly after Pann was settled back in her bed. 'She just wanted to get to the stuff!'

"She was probably right, but I thought to myself, *How hard some nurses become.*"

Eileen Langford: "Most of the time I felt the doctors and nurses were doing the best they could. But when awful and unnecessary things would happen to hurt Pann, I would get upset. For instance, the first morning I came to see her, she complained about the light coming through the window. The nurse just snapped at her. I was aghast. I said I was sure Pann hadn't meant to be difficult, and I wondered where the great spirit of encouragement I'd always felt in rehab had gone to. The nurse snapped back, 'It's still here!' and marched out of the room. As I look back now, I believe the real problem was that they all loved Pann. She had been there so much, and they had become emotionally involved with her, and now she seemed to be dying. They couldn't handle it. I think they tried to disassociate themselves for their own protection."

Pann: "The seizures continued through Christmas even though I was no longer on the Demerol. They kept giving me other medications, but they were ineffective. I now believe this was because the seizures had become functional. The first few were undoubtedly physically induced, but after a while I honestly think the seizures became the outward expression of all the anger I had allowed to build up inside me. The way I had handled my illness up to that time had not been normal or healthy. I should have been hopping mad, but instead I held it all inside, and you just can't push explosive feelings down indefinitely. All those negative emotions churning within me built up a head of steam that inevitably had to erupt. And of course the drugs didn't help. They only numbed me, making it possible to avoid dealing with my real feelings. They solved an immediate problem only to create a far more dangerous one.

"The weeks before Christmas were unreal. I was so sick that I couldn't even feed myself. Susan Flanagan, a woman I taught school with and a great friend, would come over to sit with me. She'd say, 'You'd better eat, or I'll just shovel it in,' and she would. But I didn't care. I didn't care about anything. She and my mom tried to cheer me up by making my room look Christmasy, but it didn't matter to me."

Eileen Langford: "Pann *was* difficult. She was so out of it; she wasn't herself at all. At Christmas she didn't want her room decorated, but we went ahead and put up some decorations anyway.

"Bill did the sweetest thing. He bought Pann a beautiful yellow jump suit and wrapped it up with a big bow. After she opened it, he made her get up and put it on. There was going to be a Christmas program, and he said, 'We're all going to go up and listen.' I was scared to death that Pann would have a seizure in front of everybody, but Bill got a wheelchair and put Pann in it, and we all went. K.C. too. It surprised everyone, because Pann had virtually refused to leave her room for a long time. And praise God, she stayed for the whole program and didn't have a seizure. I thought Bill was so wonderful. Instead of buying her something practical, he gave her something to flatter her femininity and make her feel like a woman again.

"As December came to an end, Pann was still out of control with the seizures. Fed up with the whole situation, Bill finally took things in hand and contacted a friend at USC who arranged to have Pann admitted to UCLA medical center. It was at this time that two very special people came into her life."

XVIII

THE MOVE TO UCLA seemed like Pann's last hope. Everyone who saw Pann knew that she was close to death, whether the doctors admitted it or not. The medical center offered the most sophisticated equipment and the most experienced minds available in the area of seizures, and if they couldn't find an answer, no one could.

During much of this time, Pann's cousin Phyllis took care of K.C. Watching the bright-eyed two-year-old laugh and play with his older cousins or curled up like a sleeping angel in bed at night, her heart would break at the thought that he might soon be motherless. Many times during the day, Phyllis would fight back tears of grief and repeatedly ask God the question that plagued them all: Why?

A couple of days before Pann was scheduled to go to UCLA, Phyllis was sitting at the kitchen table having a good cry when she felt the Holy Spirit direct her to the Bible.

Opening it at random, she let her eyes fall on the page. The words "she can yet be healed" jumped out at her. Blinking to clear away her tears, she read the entire verse (Jeremiah 51:8 LB): "Weep for her; give her medicine; perhaps she can yet be healed." This time tears of joy filled Phyllis's eyes. She rushed to the phone.

A chill ran down Pann's spine as she listened to her cousin's excited explanation of the Scripture that God had given her. She had been through too much to be hopeful, but this was the first sign in a long time that God had not forgotten her. Maybe the move to UCLA *would* make a difference.

But once there, Pann's spirits plummeted. A new battery of tests proved inconclusive, and a new team of unfamiliar doctors began the old and all-too-familiar guessing games. When the seizures continued, she dismissed Phyllis's encouragement as little more than wishful thinking. Nothing had changed. The only difference was that shortly after her arrival it was discovered that light could trigger her seizures, so now she lived in a state of perpetual darkness, unable to read, watch TV, or even look out the window.

Imprisoned by darkness and pain, it was nearly impossible for Pann to remember the person she had once been or the life she had known. She knew that eons ago she had loved life and cared about others, but that was another place and another time. That was a world of sunlight and laughter, full of hope and possibilities; a world where nightmares ended when you woke in the morning and prayers were answered if you had the faith of a mustard seed.

"That must be my problem," she confided to Herb Downie in a voice that bespoke her defeat. "I just don't have enough strength to believe that God's really going to do anything for me. I mean, all it takes is the faith of a mustard seed, and I don't even have that anymore! I've lost it, and I don't know how to get it back!"

Dr. Downie sat quietly for a few moments, praying that God would give him something to say. While Dr. Downie had sat with many people faced with pain and imminent death, he had a special affection for Pann and Bill. He had watched them both grow up at Hollywood Presbyterian Church. He had seen Pann go from an awkward girl in braces to a lovely young wife and mother, and his feelings for her made him all the more desperate to give her a glimmer of hope. Then he had a thought.

"You know that big, old purse you used to carry everywhere? Bill used to say you carried everything *including* the kitchen sink in it! Remember?" Dr. Downie laughed.

"Yes, I remember," Pann responded, wondering what possible significance her old purse could have.

"Well, it seems to me that you used to have a hard time finding your keys in that big old bag. You'd run around looking for them, telling everybody that you'd lost your keys. Pretty soon we'd all be looking. But more times than not, you would finally dump the purse out on the floor and there they'd be, down at the very bottom, lost among all the junk. I think it's the same thing with your faith right now, Pann. You haven't really lost it. It's just buried under so much junk you can't find it. If you could empty your purse, you'd find it was there all along, just like the keys."

Tears streamed down Pann's cheeks as she grabbed Dr. Downie's hand. His simple illustration was exactly what she needed. It made so much sense. Of course her faith was still there, but how was she going to find it? How could she "empty her purse?"

Pann had no way of knowing that God was in the process of sending someone with the answer to that question. Lois Bock had known Pann and her family for years. Her husband, Fred, a well-known writer and director of gospel music, had worked with the choirs at Hollywood Presbyterian Church. Consequently, the Bocks were good friends of Dick and Eileen Langford and knew all about Pann and Bill.

Lois: "But we were never close friends with the Baltzes until God chose to throw us into the middle of their situation. In fact, I didn't know Pann very well, but I was aware of her problems. Our entire church had been praying for her since the first stroke, and by the time she started having seizures, I was really beginning to wonder what was wrong. Why wasn't God answering our prayers? Pann's problems highlighted questions about my own personal walk, and I found myself struggling over the whole issue of whether God actually does answer prayer.

"During this time I was invited to speak at a conference in Indianapolis. At a speakers' dinner I was assigned a seat next to a woman I had never met or heard of before. Her name was Glaphré* Gilliland, and she was as unusual-looking as her name. Tall and big boned, there is no way to describe her but *plain*, both in feature and dress. My first thought was, *Wonderful! I have absolutely nothing in common with this woman. What are we going to talk about?* But since I knew no one else at the table, I opened a conversation by asking about her ministry.

" 'God has called me to teach others about the power of prayer. I call it Prayerlife,' Glaphré responded with immediate warmth and candor.

" 'Oh?' I said, my interest suddenly piqued. 'Tell me more.'

"Glaphré went on to tell me how God had led her, step by step, into a walk of total dependency and faith in Him, teaching her to hear His voice in even the smallest situations. When she had finished, I told her how interesting it was that I was sitting next to her, because I was probably at the lowest point in my life

_____
*Pronounced "GLAY-free."

concerning prayer. I went on to tell her all about Pann. 'So there she is,' I finished, 'with a little boy, a husband who loves her, and family and friends who are praying. But it's like everyone's prayers are hitting the ceiling, because God just doesn't choose to make a difference in Pann's life.'

" 'Believe me, I understand,' Glaphré responded quietly. 'I have a terminal illness God has chosen not to heal, and I know how hard it can be to continue believing God loves you when the answer is no.'*

"During the rest of the meal, Glaphré tried to help me see that sometimes God doesn't answer prayer the way we want Him to or on our time schedule. But she assured me that our prayers certainly had gone beyond ceiling level and that one day we would see the answer.

"A few days after Christmas, the phone rang. It was Glaphré calling from her home in Oklahoma. She told me that she had been snowed in for a couple of days and that God had directed her to spend the time praying for Pann. She felt the Lord really wanted to say something to Pann, and she wanted to know if I would be the messenger.

" 'Pann really needs some deep inner healing. I want you to pray through her life with her, a few years at a time. First, have her describe where she was and her family situation at the time to give you some direction. Then both of you pray silently, asking God to shine a spotlight of revelation and healing into her life, to expose anything that needs to be dealt with. Then pray with her for those things.'

"My immediate response was, 'Wait a minute! You're asking the wrong person. Prayer is *your* ministry, not mine! I've never done anything like this. I would feel very good about

*Glaphré's story can be found in her book *When the Pieces Don't Fit*. She also wrote *Talking With God*, in which she outlines her method of private and group prayer. Both books are published by Zondervan Publishing House.

having you fly out here to do it, but *I* can't do it. It simply isn't my gift. I have other gifts, and I am faithful with those, but this is not one of them!'

"Glaphré replied, 'I can't fly out, and I really felt certain that I was getting the right message from God. But if you don't feel comfortable about it, then obviously you're not to do it. I just needed to throw it out and leave it with you as to what to do with it. I'm sure whatever you decide will be right.'

"Later, I told my husband, Fred, about the conversation. 'There is just no way I can go to Pann and do this,' I said. 'This is not the kind of thing I do.'

"Fred said, 'Well, whatever you think.'

"'I mean,' I continued as though *he* needed to be convinced, 'how can I just walk in there and tell her that she needs to go through her life with me—a virtual stranger—and reveal her past hurts and failures? I know I wouldn't like it if someone came to me with that suggestion!'

"'Okay, honey. No one is going to put a gun to your head and make you do something you don't want to do. Glaphré didn't insist, did she? You do what you feel is right,' Fred replied, echoing Glaphré's sentiments.

"But I couldn't get the idea out of my mind. I thought about it every minute for several days. Finally Fred asked what I was so afraid of. I answered honestly, 'She's very ill. If I do or say something wrong, I could push her right over the edge, emotionally. I've never done anything like this before. I don't know what to do. What if God isn't in it? What if I try and it's just me there, messing around in Pann's life?'

"He said, 'I think I'd trust Glaphré and what God is saying *through* her.'

"I spent the rest of the night praying about whether or not I should do it. I kept hearing Glaphré's voice saying, 'I felt certain I was getting the right message.' Still, when I said I couldn't do it, she hadn't condemned me or tried to pressure me. If she had, my defenses would have gone sky high. Instead, her total acceptance and love had left me open and free to be available to the leading of the Holy Spirit, and in my quiet time before the Lord, I knew not only that I needed to do it, but that I would answer to God if I didn't. I called Pann the next morning to ask if I could come see her."

Lois's call came as a complete surprise to Pann, who agreed to the visit with a mixture of curiosity and dread. Pann's emotions were still stinging from one well-meaning person's suggestion that Pann was being punished for unconfessed sin, and she couldn't help but wonder just what new "words of encouragement" Lois would bring.

Lois: "I was very nervous the first day I went to see Pann. She looked so depressed and fragile. All these tubes were attached for intravenous feedings because her mouth was so raw she couldn't eat anything. The greatest surprise was the darkness. I didn't know before I went that light could trigger a seizure, and as I started to tell her about Glaphré, the message I brought took on an entirely new meaning. Here I was, sitting in a pitch-dark room telling Pann that God wanted her to expose herself to the one thing she feared most—light. Later she told me that the reference to light was the thing that convinced her God was speaking.

"We started a couple of days later, taking the early years five at a time, then two at a time as we got to her teens. I came two or three days a week, and it was remarkable to see her change as the searchlight of the Holy Spirit started to illuminate painful areas."

Pann and Lois had no idea what to expect when they first bowed their heads and invited the Holy Spirit to begin revealing areas of hurt that needed to be healed. After all, they were novices, stepping out in simple obedience, with no real sense of direction beyond the first step. When the first clear memory popped into Pann's head, she felt hesitant to even speak it because it seemed so silly and unimportant.

"I was three years old," she began, feeling her face flush with embarrassment. "I'd had my tonsils taken out, and my mother came to the hospital with a basket containing a beautiful stuffed cat with three baby kittens made out of rabbit fur." Pann hesitated. "I feel really stupid telling you this. It's just—well—I really loved those kittens." Pann's voice broke, and she had to let the unexpected rush of emotion pass before she could continue. "They were so soft and cuddly. I played with them, slept with them, gave them all names. . . ." As Pann spoke, an old forgotten pain began to rise from somewhere deep within. It became more and more difficult for her to squeeze the words out through the pain.

"Go on," Lois encouraged softly.

"After I came home from the hospital, my mother discovered the cats had become infested with maggots. She had to take them away from me and burn them." By this time tears were streaming down Pann's cheeks; her body shook with the outraged sobs of an innocent confronted for the first time with the inequities of life and the pain of loss. "This seems so dumb. I'm a grownup. I understand why she had to do it. But then I couldn't understand how she could take something that meant so much to me and burn it. I felt so betrayed. I mourned for those cats for years—but I never said anything about it until now."

Lois held Pann while she relived the pain of that little girl and shed the tears that had been bottled up inside her for nearly twenty-five years. Then, as Pann's sobs subsided, Lois prayed for a deep and final healing of that old festering wound. It was such a simple thing, but as Lois ended her prayer, Pann felt the warmth of peace begin to glow in the icy depths of her soul.

Through the weeks that followed, that healing warmth spread further as, year by year, memory by memory, Pann released to the Savior the pain of long-forgotten rejections, disappointments, and failures. Some were major wounds that felt like a sword to the heart. Others were more like splinters left to fester in her soul, overlooked before as insignificant.

Later, when Lois and Pann were ready to deal with the years of her illness, Bill joined them. For the first time, Pann faced the unspoken hurts and fears that had crippled her emotions as the strokes had crippled her body. Loneliness, for example. No one could possibly understand how lonely Pann had been, locked within the prison of her illness. How could anyone know how she felt as she watched Bill and K.C. walk out the door after a visit, leaving her behind, alone? Even at home there was a constant awareness that she was different. She felt as if someone had slapped a sticker on her back that read, *Fragile! Handle With Care!* Yet even with all the special handling, something always managed to break, and she would find herself back in the loneliest place of all—the battle for survival. No one could crawl inside and help her fight—not Bill, not her mother or father, not the doctors. But there was One who had fought death and won, the same One who now came to comfort and heal her. As Lois and Pann talked and prayed, the knowledge of that truth gradually became more than a life preserver for Pann to cling to; it became a rock upon which she could stand and rest and find refuge.

Lois: "Pann seemed to improve every time I saw her. One Saturday night I was in the kitchen fixing dinner when the phone rang. In a little voice, Pann said, 'Lois, you told me that if I ever wanted something, you would bring it to me.'

" 'Sure. What would you like?' I responded, thinking she wanted me to bring her something the next time I came.

" 'Well, the doctor was just in here, and he said that I could have anything I want to eat. And what I want is a number eleven from Hamburger Hamlet, onion rings, and a Coke.'

" 'Are you sure the doctor said you could have that?' I asked, not believing my ears.

" 'Yes, I can have it.'

" 'Well, okay. I'll get it to you.' I hung up the phone and turned to Fred. 'I've got to go to UCLA. Pann wants a number eleven, onion rings, and a Coke from Hamburger Hamlet.'

" 'What!' he choked in surprise. 'I thought you said she's on intravenous feedings.'

" 'She was, but the doctor said she can have whatever she wants to eat, and that's what she wants. She certainly can't get it herself, so I'm going to get it for her.'

" 'Lois, it's Saturday night. You'll never find a place to park. Better let me drive you over there. I can drive around the block while you run in and get the hamburger.' Fred sighed, resigning himself to joining in my madness.

"So I turned off the burners on the stove, and we drove out to UCLA, got the hamburger, and took it to Pann. Then Fred and I sat on the bed and marveled as Pann devoured every bite.

"As we got in the car to go home, I said to Fred, 'I think we've made a gigantic mistake. You don't go straight from intravenous feedings to onion rings. She will be sick all night.'

"I didn't sleep a wink that night. I kept waking up thinking of poor Pann deathly ill because of my stupidity. I could barely wait for morning so I could call and see if she was all right.

" 'Oh, I'm just fine,' she answered cheerily when I got her on the phone. 'I had a terrific night! Slept straight through!'

136

"'Oh,' I answered through a yawn. 'Well, I'm certainly glad *one* of us did.'

"That was the first major sign that Pann was doing better. During the time we prayed together, I saw her change from a fragile, depressed, despondent little thing to a person who suddenly went back to having pride in the way she looked. She became independent again, getting out of bed and washing her hair. I would walk in and find her sitting up in bed with her hair done and earrings on. She looked totally different from the person whose haunted, desperate face had greeted me that first day. I saw her regain some of her old spunk. And best of all, the seizures were becoming less severe."

About two weeks after Lois and Pann began praying, blood tests revealed that Pann was extremely toxic. The drugs that had been prescribed to help her were literally poisoning her system, perhaps even causing the very seizures they were intended to control. She was taken off all medication, and within a few days the seizures stopped. They never returned.

"A heart at peace gives life to the body" (Proverbs 14:30).

XIX

C EASE TO DWELL on days gone by or to brood over past history. Here and now I will do a new thing; this moment it will break from the bud. Can you not perceive it? I will make a way even through the wilderness and paths in the barren desert" (Isaiah 43:18–19 NEB).

Pann read the words quietly to herself. The verses were a needed reminder to look toward the future and not dwell on the nightmare of the past. God most surely had made a way through the barren wilderness of the past year, and they had all come through. During 1976 she had been in the hospital more than nine months, and there had been many days when she feared she would never again sit in her own living room, relaxed and free from pain, sipping a cup of hot tea and listening to K.C.'s happy chatter. But that's exactly what she was doing. She left the hospital at the end of January; it was now the middle of March. She had the use of both arms and was walking fairly well with the help of a brace and a cane. She was driving and cooking and shopping on her own, and the person that looked back at her in the mirror was actually beginning to look familiar again.

Best of all, the work of emotional healing that God had begun in the hospital was continuing—and now included Bill as well.

Seeing how God had been tenderly dealing with Pann made Bill aware of many areas of hurt in his own life, so he and Pann began meeting with Lois and Fred to pray through the years of Pann's illness. Two areas that God immediately dealt with were Bill's guilt and anger. He felt guilty because he was healthy while Pann was ill. He felt guilty *and* angry because he was her husband, her protector, and her covering, yet he couldn't do anything to make her well. And he was angry with Pann for putting him into a position of inadequacy. He was also hurt by Pann's occasional insensitivity to the gigantic effort it took him to simply stand firm, work hard, remain faithful, and be supportive, not only to her, but also to the rest of the family who was devastated by this illness. Bill, the provider. Bill, the decision maker. Bill, the encourager and comforter. Bill, the rock upon whom everyone leaned. No one knew how exhausting it was being a rock, and occasionally Bill would surprise himself with an unexpected burst of anger toward Pann, who once again was pressing him to his limit with yet another stroke or emergency.

Then as sure as ebb follows flow, the guilt would rush in to wash away his anger and leave him feeling even more inadequate than he had before. And so the cycle went.

The sessions with the Bocks gave Bill the opportunity to express feelings he had repressed for years. The act of exposing the bruised side of his soul to the healing balm of God's Spirit broke the vicious cycle of anger, guilt, and hurt and allowed healing to begin. It also opened new lines of communication between Pann and Bill.

Pann: "It was important for us to understand that anger is a natural by-product of a long and critical illness. The person who is sick is going to lash out in frustration and fear, and even feel resentment because those around her are healthy and pain-free. And the family will occasionally be angry at the person who is sick. It's all part of the normal response, and you must be able to confront those feelings in an honest and constructive way. I think a lot of relationships split up because there is so much guilt about how people are feeling. I honestly don't know where Bill and I would be today if God had not forced us to open up to each other. Fortunately, we were able to start being honest about our feelings with each other before God."

Pann was also continuing her therapy with Dr. Griffith. The spiritual healing she had experienced allowed her finally to deal with many feelings she had resisted facing honestly before, and her sessions with Dr. Griffith were more effective because of it.

Only one minor setback clouded the otherwise clear skies of the past two months. Pann had had stomach pains shortly after she left the hospital. The doctors suspected that a tubal ligation of the previous year was the cause. "Band-aid" surgery was performed (in which a tube is inserted through the bellybutton so that no incision is necessary) to correct some adhesions that were binding the tubal ligation to the intestines.

That should have been the end of it. But after surgery Pann's throat began to swell from the breathing tube that had been inserted during the procedure. She was put on a respirator for two days. When her condition didn't improve, another tracheostomy was put in place. That had been a month and a half earlier, and the trach was still with her.

But this time the sight of the white tube in her throat didn't make her quite as uncomfortable, and she adjusted fairly quickly. She even found herself amused by some people's responses. The week before, for instance, she had been shopping in a department store, enjoying the luxury of strolling from department to department, taking in all the bright colors and sounds, and wondering at the many changes in fashion since the last time she had looked. She felt wonderfully normal, despite the many curious stares she drew as she limped down the aisles with the white tube sticking obtrusively out of her throat. Every attempt to camouflage or hide it with a scarf had failed, and she had finally given up, determining to ignore the reactions she inspired.

But one sales clerk proved hard to ignore. Her wide eyes never left Pann's throat as she bagged the perfume Pann purchased and rang it up at the cash register. Pann took her package and gratefully fled the woman's unblinking gaze, only to discover she had left another package at the counter. Gathering up her courage and her sense of humor, she returned. "I thought I left this here," she said with a mischievous twinkle in her eye. "I believe I'd forget my head if it wasn't screwed on!" Pann managed to keep a straight face as she retrieved the parcel from the startled sales clerk and walked away. But she couldn't resist turning to catch one final glimpse of the woman, who stood rooted to the floor, staring after her with an expression of stunned disbelief.

"What's so funny?" Eileen Langford stood in the doorway looking at her daughter with undisguised affection. She had arrived the day before for a visit.

"Oh, I was just thinking about that sales clerk the other day. I guess I must be a pretty amazing sight to most people."

"Honey, you're still a lovely young woman, and as soon as you get that trach out, you'll be just fine," her mother encouraged.

"I suppose. I'm not really worried about it," said Pann, not wanting to sound discouraged. "As long as I can keep my sense of humor, I'll be all right. And Bill . . . he really made me laugh the other night. I was getting ready for bed, and I felt him staring at me. Most of the time I try not to think about the fact that my body is beginning to resemble a road map of New Jersey, but when Bill's around, it's hard not to wonder what he really thinks about all my scars. I started feeling all self-conscious and paranoid until he winked at me and called me his Battle-Scarred-Galactica. I didn't know if I should hit him or hug him!"

Mrs. Langford laughed as she poured herself a cup of tea. Then she settled on the couch to talk. "You and Bill are doing so well. I'm so proud of you both. I wish I could say the same about your father and me."

"How is Daddy?" Pann asked, knowing how hard her illness had been on him.

"I'm not sure. He doesn't talk to me much anymore. Not about the things that are really bothering him. Not about you," Mrs. Langford answered sadly. "He just can't seem to open up. I know he's hurting terribly, feeling somehow that God has let him down by allowing you to suffer as you have. As hard as he tries to be a strength to me, he doesn't realize that it would help us both if we could share our anger and grief together. Instead he just closes up and won't talk about it."

"I wish there was something I could do," said Pann. "I sometimes think that the worst part of my whole illness is the pain it causes those I love. But at least Bill and I are starting to talk about it. We actually had an old-fashioned, no-holds-barred fight the night before last. Dr. Griffith has been saying how important it is for us to honestly express our feelings to each other, both the good and the bad, instead of Bill always treating me like a piece of cracked crystal that will shatter at the least sign of stress and me always clamming up to avoid any kind of confrontation. He pointed out that sometimes a good fight is the best way to release tension and clear the air and that we both need to learn we can actually yell at each other and still love each other.

"Well, I guess we're beginning to get the message, because the other night we started getting into a touchy discussion, and I could feel myself getting angry. But instead of holding it all in and sulking for the rest of the night, I began to express what I was feeling. In fact, I got so worked up that I picked up an ashtray and slammed it down on the table so hard it broke the glass top. Both Bill and I just stared at the table. We couldn't believe our eyes. Then Bill started grinning like some crazy idiot and telling me how proud he was that I'd been able to let go like that. I started laughing, and we ended up congratulating each other on having our first real fight in over two years. Maybe that's what Daddy needs to do: break a few table tops."

"Maybe." The two women sat in thoughtful silence for a few moments. Then Mrs. Langford changed the subject to the trip to Denver Pann and K.C. were planning to make, along with Bill's parents, to visit Bill's brother, Steve, and Steve's wife, Marty. Pann had made such good medical progress that her doctors had given her permission to go, feeling a change of scenery would do her good. They were scheduled to leave the next week.

Denver was just what Pann needed. Stepping off the plane, she felt revived by the crisp, clean air that tickled her nose and put pink into her cheeks. The wide expanse of sky stretched like a shimmering blue canopy between the surrounding peaks, presenting a magnificent backdrop for this healthy, wonderful world far from the claustrophobic halls of the hospital. Pann was filled with an illusion of strength and vitality as she grabbed

K.C.'s hand to walk the short distance to the terminal. The trip represented a precious opportunity for mother and son to spend some quality time together, and the two shared the same childlike expression of unbridled joy and expectation.

Steve and Marty had a home in one of Denver's rural suburbs. A thick blanket of white snow still covered the front yard. Three-year-old K.C. kept the entire family entertained with his constant expressions of amazement and delight as time and again he'd scoop up a handful of icy crystals, only to have them disappear like magic in his hand. He also found a real soulmate in his cousin, Kim. The two youngsters spent their days happily exhausting themselves by sliding, running, and rolling in the snow. They came in each afternoon looking like the Littlest Snowman and his bride.

A week later, Pann was feeling fine, eating well, and sleeping at night. One afternoon she even helped to create the most magnificent snowman this side of the Rocky Mountains. She cheered the others on to bigger and better snowballs and personally saw to it that his hat sat at just the right angle and that his eyes didn't cross.

The next morning Pann was helping with breakfast when the room suddenly began to tilt in a frighteningly familiar way. Walking unsteadily into the bathroom, she checked her reflection in the mirror. What she saw confirmed her worst fears. Her face was already beginning to droop, and the pressure in her head was increasing by the minute. It was her fifth stroke. The snowman watched in desolate silence as paramedics carried her to the ambulance. By the time she was admitted to the intensive care unit of the Swedish Medical Center in Englewood, she had lost the ability to speak and her right side was nearly paralyzed.

XX

THE HORROR PANN FELT at experiencing another stroke was compounded by her terror at being stranded in a strange place at the mercy of doctors who knew nothing about her or her history.

After her condition stabilized, Bill's parents flew back to Los Angeles with K.C. Pann knew it was better for him to be home with Bill, but she still felt an unbearable pang of grief as she watched him being carried out of her room after the brief good-bye visit. Now she was truly alone—helpless and vulnerable. She couldn't even form words to pray or lift her hand to wipe away the tears streaming down her face. Then quietly, as if in answer to her silent cries, she felt the presence of God wrap itself around her like strong, protective arms, and she was comforted by the reassurance that she was not alone.

It soon became clear that Pann was not in Denver by chance. The doctors there had no preconceived ideas to keep them from exploring all possibilities. For the first time in a long time, she heard the suggestion that her heart might be the troublemaker. The latest research indicated a definite link between mitral-leaflet prolapse and stroke, and these doctors felt in Pann's case it was a theory worth investigating.

During her second week in the hospital, Pann was moved to the tenth-floor rehabilitation unit. The stroke had once again left her right arm and leg useless, but her spirits bounced back with a buoyancy that demonstrated the deep work of renewal God had done in her life. Using her left hand, she wrote to Bill:

> I'm okay and don't want you to worry. Things aren't moving very well, but I'm not hurting except for the trach and my eyes a little. Most important is that my spirits are good. Remember that passage from Isaiah where God promises to make a way even through the wilderness, and paths through barren desert? He will and *is* doing that for me. The hardest part was sending K.C. home. I miss him so much, and we had such a special time! But I knew he would be secure and happy with Phyllis and you. I want what's best for him. And it frees Steve and Marty to visit me. Their visits have helped so much.
>
> You stay there and get caught up at work and spend time with K.C. I know you care and would come if I asked, but I'll need you more when I come home.

But Pann was not to see home again for many weeks. She had been in rehab only a few days when she suffered another setback. One minute she was sitting in her wheelchair, trying to summon the energy to begin her exercises, and the next she was on the floor, surrounded by people desperately trying to keep her alive. Her breathing had stopped. A bag was attached to her trach to pump air into her lungs while her chest was massaged to stimulate the breathing reflex. Within minutes the physician in charge of her case was on the scene, giving her a thorough going over. Checking her eyes, he discovered a number of small clots.

Pann had suffered another stroke, and this one had sent a shower of emboli, or clots, to her eyes. She was immediately rushed to the ICU and started on blood thinners. She was also put on a respirator, since she was unable to breathe on her own. She remained on the respirator for the next four weeks.

This stroke was far more damaging than the one that had put her in the hospital in the first place, and it caused the doctors to consider more seriously the desirability of open-heart surgery to replace her prolapsed valve. Next time, a shower of emboli might shoot to a more critical area of her brain and kill her or paralyze her completely.

The main problem was that Pann's heart was extremely small. The pig valve, considered best for use in a human, was too big, and plastic valves clotted easily and were risky even in the best of circumstances. But it was obvious that Pann could not survive long unless something was done, and the doctors spent the next several weeks weighing the pros and cons. Dr. Martin flew in from Los Angeles, and once again an army of people throughout the country went to their knees on Pann's behalf.

Cut off from her immediate family, Pann was grateful for the support of a growing circle of new friends. Steve and Marty were faithful visitors, and their church took Pann to heart, interceding for her in prayer and regularly sending people to visit. She also discovered a real friend in Anne Yelkin, one of her nurses. Anne always had a smile and a word of encouragement as she emptied Pann's bedpan or helped her roll over for one more jab of the needle. And Bob, the hospital chaplain, seemed to be there whenever Pann was in particular need of a shoulder to cry on or a listening ear.

Still, the days were long and often lonely as Pann fought to regain some of the ground she had lost. The stroke had robbed her of speech, and the respirator made physical therapy impossible. Fortunately, after a couple of weeks she was able to breathe on her own for as much as an hour or two at a time, enabling her to begin work with a speech therapist.

Her right arm and leg, however, remained almost useless, which made it difficult for Pann to write or do anything creative to pass the time. Her cubicle in ICU didn't even have a window. As she lay hour after hour with nothing to do but watch TV, she began to think she might fool them all by dying of boredom.

One day Steve and Marty brought their daughter, Kim, to visit. The little girl marched through the door carrying a big paper bag, which she presented to her aunt with great importance. Inside Pann found a coloring book and a big box of crayons. "Thought you might like something to do," Steve said with a smile that reminded her of Bill.

"Perfect! I love it!" Pann penned awkwardly, her artist's heart delighting in the simple gift. Her left hand could handle this simple assignment quite easily, and it would give her something to fill the empty hours while bringing a little color back into her life.

For Bill, Pann's distant hospitalization created an entirely different set of problems. He struggled to deal with the ever-increasing complications of her illness while keeping up with the daily demands of work and life in general. Hospital visitation now meant packing a suitcase and flying to Denver on weekends. He and K.C. became regulars on the two-and-a-half-hour flight, making the trip three times during the month of April. Not having Pann close enough to visit on a daily basis was a strangely terrifying feeling for Bill. What if something happened? What if she needed him and he couldn't get to her in time? Each Friday Bill would arrive hoping to hear the doctors say they had decided on a plan of action and that Pann would be coming home soon. Each Sunday he would fly home, his stomach churning with disappointment and worry over the doctors' increasing concern that Pann would never survive open-heart surgery. This worry, combined with the many daily pressures, soon began to take its toll, and Bill lost many hours of sleep and thirty pounds trying to juggle all the balls without dropping any.

Pann was having a blue day. She had been staring at the blank walls of her windowless room for over three weeks. She swore that if she lived to see K.C. grow up, she would never allow him to stick any helpless creature in a shoe box with nothing but a few punched holes to let in the sunlight and fresh air. They had taken her off the respirator a few minutes before, and she could feel her lungs working to expand with each breath as her body learned to function on its own once again. As she lay in bed mindlessly watching the images on the television set, her mouth began to work, opening and closing, stretching this way and that as her lips and tongue curled around the different sounds that were still difficult for her to articulate. Her speech was returning fairly quickly now that she was able to have speech therapy, although occasionally a word still escaped her and there was no question that this time her recovery had been slower and harder.

"Pann?"

Pann turned listlessly to look at the large, raw-boned woman who stood smiling at her from the door. "Hello, Pann," the woman said, extending her hand and moving across the room with large, confident steps. "I'm . . ."

"Glaphré." Pann finished the sentence, grabbing the offered hand with her good left one. "I'd know you anywhere," Pann continued in her whispery voice, delighted to finally meet the person God had used so powerfully in her life. "I can't believe you're here! What are you doing here?"

"I'm on my way to speak at a conference in Montana. But I had to stop in Denver for a day, and when I heard you were here, I wanted to see how you're doing."

The next hour passed quickly as Pann and Glaphré talked like old friends with much to catch up on. Much too soon, it was time for Glaphré to leave. As she stood, she asked if Pann would mind if she prayed for her. Pann readily agreed, and the two women held hands and bowed their heads. Glaphré's prayer was simple and to the point. First she praised God for being all He is: kind and loving, compassionate and forgiving, all-knowing and all-powerful. She thanked God for Pann and Bill and K.C., and for all their lives meant as a family who loved and needed one another. Then she finished her prayer by asking God, if it be His will, to please put into *her* body all of Pann's illness and pain, so that Pann could be restored to her family in wholeness and health.

Pann sat in awed silence, too moved to speak, and contemplated the face of this woman—this stranger—who had offered herself as a sacrifice on Pann's behalf. Pann had no doubt that Glaphré was sincere. She knew God was fully capable of taking her at her word and doing as she asked. As she gave Pann a hug and stood to leave, there was nothing about Glaphré's expression or manner that suggested she had done anything extraordinary. Still choked with emotion, Pann stammered for the right words, but there were none adequate to express how deeply she had been touched by Glaphré's visit and prayer. Instead, she simply thanked her new friend for coming and told her to bundle up when she reached Montana. They were having a late winter, and the news had been full of stories about the bitter cold.

"As a matter of fact," lamented Glaphré with an embarrassed laugh, "I left my heavy coat on a chair at home. I didn't even realize I didn't have it until I was on the plane. But not to worry. My God provides even when I forget my coat!" Glaphré walked to the door, then added, "I fly back through here in about a week. I'll come see you then."

After Glaphré left, Pann couldn't stop thinking about her braving the Montana cold in her thin suit jacket. "Lord," she prayed a little self-consciously, "I don't usually bother You with little requests like this, but please give Glaphré a coat."

Pann never hesitated to go to the throne of God with important problems. But like so many of us, she had divided life into two categories: those things we can take care of ourselves and those things for which we need God's help. It had never occurred to her that God desired to be included in the countless small, nitty-gritty problems and decisions that make up ninety percent of our lives. Still, she was filled with an unexpected excitement wanting to see what God would do.

A week later, when Glaphré came by again as promised, the first thing Pann asked her was, "Did you find a coat?"

"God took good care of me," Glaphré declared with a grin. "When I stepped off the airplane, *five* different people promptly offered me a coat. It seems they all got the same idea as they were leaving for the airport to meet me. They just had a *feeling* that I might not have a warm coat with me, since I was coming from Oklahoma. And the amazing thing is," Glaphré added, patting her ample frame, "they all fit!"

XXI

GLAPHRÉ'S VISITS did much to lift Pann's spirits during the days leading up to Easter. She received another boost a few days later when she was informed that she could finally be moved from the windowless side of ICU to a room with a big picture window. Pann felt as though she were being released from prison when she left the dark little cell for the last time and was wheeled down the hall to her new room. Crossing the threshold, she gasped with surprise. The entire room was decorated like a scene out of *Peter Rabbit Has an Easter Party*. Pink, yellow, and blue streamers were everywhere, crisscrossing her bed and hanging from the ceiling and mirror. Even the IV stand was wrapped like a skinny Maypole. Colorful eggs filled a big basket by her bed, and paper bunnies peered cheerily out of every corner.

"I don't believe it!" Pann squealed, clapping her hands in delight. "Who did this?"

"Me. Surprised?" said the tall, slender young woman bursting out from behind the door like a small whirlwind of laughter and fun.

"Sonia! I thought you left!"

Sonia Evans was a friend from Los Angeles. Since her husband was a commercial airline pilot, she had used her family-fare privilege to fly to Denver for the day to visit Pann. When she learned of Pann's room change, she raced madly all over town, collecting Easter goodies to give her friend this special surprise. Such expressions of love helped keep Pann from despairing completely when she moved a week later to the rehab ward and prepared to tackle again the strenuous chore of physical rehabilitation.

The first thing Pann noticed about this rehab ward was how young many of the patients were. She was used to the older people, usually stroke victims like herself, who worked to reeducate paralyzed limbs and clumsy tongues. But this hospital was well-known for its work with trauma victims. Everywhere you looked, there were young men and women whose bodies had been mangled in accidents that had left them scarred and often without an arm or a leg. In the midst of this it was easy to be overwhelmed by negative feelings, and Pann had to dig hard and deep to draw on the well-spring of hope God had given her. She wrote:

> I was just up for the first time on the parallel bars, trying to take my first steps since my last stroke. It was an incredible effort to try to keep my balance and to pull the right leg through. When we had finished I was crying. The physical therapist didn't understand. She had thought that I would feel happy to be up, but the frustration of trying to make a leg move that does not want to move brought back memories of all the times I have been in this same position, and I was overwhelmed by feelings of discouragement. I want to be able to stand up and walk across the room right

now, but I know how much time and effort it will take before I am able to do that. And all the doubts as to just how far I'll get before I lose it again crowd in to make me feel it is not worth trying anymore. I'd just rather spend the time at home.

Then, when I'm finished feeling sorry for myself, I feel guilty because I'm so very lucky in comparison with the others here. *Lord, forgive me for only seeing the negative. But thank You for understanding how I feel. Take my small faith and teach me to trust Your plans for my good, and help me to live one day at a time.*

Being thrust into the harsh reality of the rehabilitation ward was both a blessing and a curse for Pann. It definitely put her problems into perspective by dramatically illustrating how bad "bad" can be. But she was not emotionally prepared to deal with the ugly, naked pain all around her. The first few days she was shocked by the sight of a teenage motorcycle-accident victim trying to take his first painful steps on an artificial limb that chafed the still red and tender stub that had once been his leg. And she had to avert her eyes from the painfully distorted mask that had at one time been the face of a young burn victim.

Still, the human spirit adapts. Soon Pann saw past the oozing sores and disfigurements to the needy spirits of people who were trying, as she was, to put their lives back together. She wanted to reach out and encourage them with the love of Jesus and the hope she had in Him. She wrote in her journal:

April 24, 1977

Good Morning, Lord,

It's a sunny Sunday morning here by the window in Denver. I've been in the hospital now for six weeks. I thought I'd write to You since it's been hard to keep my thoughts on one track to talk to You. My thoughts seem so centered on myself. Perhaps by writing I can get those out and see beyond me to You and others.

What strikes me so deeply is that I often don't know how to pray or what to ask for. I think back to the day when the doctors told me about my heart throwing clots and the poor risks of surgery. At that moment I was faced with the reality of a future with no positive choices or answers, and I was in agony of spirit. I did not know how to pray. Then it came to me so clearly how the Holy Spirit is our Comforter and speaks to God for us. My soul was in agony of communication with God, but I could not put words into sentences to speak what I felt. Yet I felt certain that God heard through my tears. The Comforter had spoken for me, and, as I told Glaphré, by morning my despair had slipped into peace, and I was able to claim the inner healing You gave me at UCLA.

I am so very homesick. I miss Bill and K.C. terribly, and it is hard to know how to best pray for them. I liked how Glaphré asked You to be a good mother to K.C. It is so easy to see Your love in K.C.'s good spirits and happy nature and in his excitement in talking to me. And I see Bill loving and missing me and feeling (physically) better, and these are also signs of Your love to me.

Keep us a true family of love, although we are apart. Give us patience to wait to be reunited. Help us feel Your love each second in all things. And please, Lord, open the right doors of decision for us.

Deciding what to do next was a frustrating process, fraught with contradictions and endless questions. The only thing that became clearer with each passing day was that doing nothing was a dangerous course of action.

After visiting their daughter in the hospital and talking with her doctors, the Langfords asked Bill if he would mind if they did some checking on their own. Years before, Dick Langford had performed the wedding ceremony of a young woman named Roma Shabaglian and her fiancé, Dr. Jeremy Swan. Jeremy was now the chief of cardiology at Cedars-Sinai Hospital in Los Angeles, and Pann's father felt that if anyone would know what to do next, he would.

Dr. Langford reached Jeremy as he was getting ready to leave for South America to give a series of lectures. He had only fifteen minutes before he had to leave to catch his plane, but he took the time to ascertain the pertinent facts of Pann's case and recommend that she go to a certain major medical clinic that handled a lot of strange and difficult cases. He also offered to call a friend at that clinic, to see if he could get her admitted. A few minutes later he called back. The answer was yes. Now all that was needed was the proper recommendations from Dr. Martin and to wait for the doctors in Denver to decide what they were going to do.

April 25, 1977

Dear Lord,

If the heart doctors can make it, today should be a big day of decision. After the results of my latest tests, I am pretty sure that they will say no to open heart surgery for a new valve, even though You know I want the operation. I am confident You will preserve my life through the many risks, and I am tired of hospitals, of being sick, and of being away from K.C. and Bill. I think it is worth the risks for the chance it might give me for a normal life. But I know from the past that Yours is the complete wisdom and often when something I have wanted desperately has gone the other way, I have looked back and seen Your complete wisdom and plan.

What I ask is that You open the minds of the doctors to do the surgery *if* this is part of Your best plan for my life and would give me the best chance for better health. If this is not Your best plan, I ask that You make it clear to me that the door is closed.

April 26, 1977

We did not make a decision yesterday. The doctors cannot come until tomorrow. I feel peaceful about the meeting.

I am also faced with a decision about the clinic. You know how opposed I have been to going that far away from home, but now it seems as if doors are opening in that direction. Part of me is still very homesick and wants to see my loved ones and forget all this. Still, I leave the decision up to You. If You want me there, make it so that it is the only way I can see to go.

Thank You, Lord, for friends like Anne and Chaplain Bob, Steve, Marty, and Kim. I praise You for the beauty outside the windows that refreshes my spirits and for the signs of daily life (smoke from chimneys, cars moving, kites flying) that make me feel part of a normal existence. Most of all, thank You for Your gift of inner healing—for the peace within me, for the release that comes with tears, for being able to express myself.

The thing I'm just beginning to learn is the importance of claiming the healing I have been given and having confidence that the healing remains despite the attacks of Satan. My tendency has been to feel that because I have had times of fear and despair, God really hasn't healed me. But by claiming that healing and telling God of the hurt and despair and claiming His peace, I feel—and more importantly *know*—it is real.

May 6

Thank You, Lord! I am writing with my right hand!

Daddy comes today, and tomorrow we are off to the clinic. Thank You for opening the doors. Daddy once told Bill when he was considering the ministry as a vocation that he should not commit himself to it unless it was the only door open to him. I believe God works to guide us by opening and closing doors. When it came to the decision here about open-heart surgery, Chaplain Bob helped me to pray that open and shut doors would guide my decision. Knowing the doctors were negative already, I asked God to open the doors of their minds if it was what He wanted. If it was not His will for my best, then I asked that He would make it clear to me that the doors were closed and help me to accept that. He did make it clear that the doors were shut.

In deciding on the clinic, my mind was definitely closed. But my family wanted me to go, and Dr. Swan recommended that I go, and God began to open my mind. Daddy and I prayed that if God wanted me to go, all the doctors would agree. Knowing that doctors *never* agree on anything, I thought I'd be safe. But a miracle happened and the doctors all agreed, opening a door that had always been closed before. The violent objections I had vanished as God freely opened the door of my will, as well.

God works through doors.

XXII

L EAVING FOR THE CLINIC the next day, Pann felt like Dorothy skipping off to the Emerald City in search of the great wizard who would give her the answer to her problem and then send her home with three clicks of her ruby bedroom slippers. Dick Langford shared his daughter's excitement and optimism. For three long years, he had been forced to stand on the sidelines and watch his only daughter fight for her life. Now he was able to take some action and, by so doing, break the bonds of guilt that had nearly strangled him in his helplessness. The outrage and sense of failure a father feels when he can't help his hurting child is soul deep and comes out of the most basic, God-imbued need to comfort and protect.

Dick Langford: "During my years as a minister it seemed that I was always defending God to those who asked me why God allows bad things to happen. Eventually I learned not to attempt to explain God to people who suffered or to those whose loved ones suffered, for I would always fail. But I believed one thing and still do: God loved them and He did not inflict suffering upon them. Of course, it was very hard to keep my perspective when I hurt so much seeing Pann suffer. Through the years I cried many times, wishing that I could take her place and knowing that I could not. But the one thing I *could* do was intervene whenever I felt she was not getting the best possible help available."

Believing that the clinic was that best help, Dick Langford asked for and received a two-month leave of absence from his church in Seattle so he could fly with Pann to the clinic and be with her.

The beautiful tree-lined streets surrounding the clinic created a parklike setting for the sprawling grounds of the central hospital where Pann was to stay. Checking in, she handed over the thick manila envelope she had carried from Denver that contained her current medical history and test results. Dr. Martin had already mailed a copy of all his records, so the clinic doctors were armed with all the available information.

Predictably, the first week was nothing more than one long test after another, as a battery of very distinguished and respected doctors took turns investigating their areas of expertise. The neurologist came first. He was an extremely officious type, treating Pann with all the warmth and compassion he would have conferred on a gerbil in the experimental lab. This first introduction to the clinic staff disheartened Pann. If her father had not been there to comfort and encourage her, she would have flown home the next day.

Instead, she stayed and met her cardiologist, who made up for the first doctor with an abundance of warmth and caring. He was a good friend of Jeremy Swan's and went out of his way to make Pann feel at ease as he put her through the usual tests, plus a few she wasn't familiar with.

Next came the ear-nose-and-throat specialist. When Pann arrived at the clinic, she was breathing through an open metal trach. To speak, she had to place her finger over the opening. The ENT man was full of ideas about new procedures that might help Pann. He told her about an experimental surgical procedure developed at UCLA that he had performed on a young girl whose cords were paralyzed like Pann's. He had separated and anchored the cords open permanently. The operation had left the girl with a rather whispery voice, but she could now breathe without a trach. He even had his young patient call Pann, to let her hear her voice. He also had Pann fitted with the newest type of trach.

Pann was so encouraged by the cardiologist and the ENT specialist that she immediately wrote Bill.

> On Wednesday Daddy and I went to the Clinic to see the throat specialist. He was super and very straight with me about what he feels is the cause of my cord paralysis and what my options are. He thinks that my cords have actually been partially paralyzed ever since last June from a clot in my brain stem at the vagus nerve. I could breathe without the trach but was not getting a full supply of oxygen, which made me very tired—like running at half-steam. That certainly describes me this past year! Now the paralysis is so severe, I don't have the option of going without a trach, and the doctor does not feel the cords will loosen.
>
> I am left with what he calls the "compromise choices" of a lifelong trach or surgery that will alter my voice. Either way my activities will be limited by not enough oxygen. If they opened my cords surgically wide enough to allow normal activity, I would not be able to talk.
>
> Speaking of talking, the doctor gave me a new trach, the Cadillac of trach tubes! It is sterling silver and has a trap

161

door that allows air in but that closes for me to talk. No more fingers in the dike!

The cardiologist here is super. He feels the heart valve is not my problem, but that I probably have a rare condition called post partum hypercoagulability, meaning that after K.C. was born, my system went haywire producing clots. My periods have accentuated the problem, but the Coumadin and Anturane I am taking should control it.

The doctors' positive attitudes were contagious. Pann began her second week at the hospital with hope and gratitude, for never before had she seen so much accomplished so quickly. She was even getting used to her neurologist's icy bedside manner. The important thing was that these men were finding answers, and soon she would be going home.

With things going so well, it was easy to relax and take advantage of the quiet, intimate hours with her father. It had been years since they had had time to do nothing but talk and enjoy each other's company. It was a special time of reestablishing old bonds and discovering new ones as they began seeing each other not only in the reflection of their past relationship, but in the reality of how they had grown and changed during the past few years.

Pann's favorite time of day was late afternoon, when her father would arrive and spend time with her. Usually Dr. Langford would push Pann's wheelchair for a long, leisurely stroll around the grounds, ending up in a picturesque courtyard with a statue of St. Francis. The artist had managed to capture an expression of great gentleness and compassion that transformed the cold marble into a figure of comfort and encouragement. Other days they would just sit out on the open porch area, watching the long, hectic day fade gradually into dusk, and Pann would search the sky for the first faint glimmer of the evening star.

"Star light, star bright, first star I see tonight, I wish I may, I wish I might . . ." Her wish was always the same.

Pann combed her hair carefully and dabbed a little more color on her cheeks. Not that she needed it. Her cheeks were already flushed with apprehension, and her stomach was full of battling butterflies as she waited for the neurologist. Something was wrong. Earlier in the day she had been called to a conference with the ENT specialist. The second she entered the room, she had sensed the change. His smile and greeting held none of the open friendliness she had come to expect. Instead, detached professionalism prevailed as he informed her that he had changed his mind about recommending her as a candidate for cord surgery at UCLA and felt the best thing she could do was go home, find a good ENT man, and work toward getting her trach out as soon as possible. He would give no explanation when she asked him why he had made this sudden one-hundred-eighty-degree turn. She felt as if a door had just been slammed in her face.

Now she glanced nervously toward the hall, willing her dad to appear. She had no idea what to expect, but she didn't want to face "Old Stoneface" alone. Dick Langford walked in with a deliberately light stride. He was as apprehensive as his daughter, but he was determined not to show it as the two waited in thoughtful silence.

When the doctor finally arrived, Pann tried to read his face. It was strangely closed and expressionless. She reached for her father's hand, steeling herself for the worst. *He's going to tell me there is nothing they can do for me. Or even worse, they have discovered something else wrong—cancer or a brain tumor. Maybe I'll be dead in a few weeks, and that's why the ENT man changed his mind.* Her mind whirled with dreadful possibilities, but never in her wildest nightmare could Pann have imagined the words about to come out of the neurologist's mouth.

"Mrs. Baltz," he began, his normally impersonal eyes looking at her with a steely expression bordering on disdain, "we have gone over all your tests thoroughly, and it is our considered opinion that there is nothing physically wrong with you. We don't believe that you have had now or have ever had in the past a real stroke. Yours is totally an emotional illness, and our best advice to you is to admit yourself to a psychiatric hospital for treatment or you may end up institutionalized."

Pann sat frozen with shock and disbelief. She felt hot waves of shame and anger wash over her, setting her cheeks ablaze and her fingers and toes tingling as though a bolt of electricity had shot through her body. Her head rang, and for a few seconds her eyes refused to focus.

The doctor continued in a carefully modulated monotone, oblivious to the impact his words were having. He explained that her brain X rays were normal, her CAT scans were normal, and while her EEG was *not* normal, he dismissed that as being of little or no significance. The important thing, in his opinion, was that her brain checked out clear. If Pann had really had a stroke, he felt convinced they would have detected some residual clotting. Since there was none, he thought it obvious that no strokes had ever occurred. Consequently, his whole manner and tone implied, his valuable time and that of his colleagues had been wasted on a wild-goose chase, and he would appreciate it if Pann would make arrangements to vacate the bed as soon as possible, so someone who was *really* sick could fill it.

Now Pann understood the ENT man's abrupt change. The others had convinced him that she was nothing more than a "head case" and that his efforts, too, had been misspent. The only doctor who remained sympathetic was Jeremy's friend, the cardiologist. Although he strongly disagreed with the diagnosis, his opinion was overruled.

That evening Pann ran the gamut of emotions. Mountainous indignation was followed by tormenting doubts and fears. *What if the doctors were right?* But even as Pann allowed the question to form in her mind, she knew they were wrong, and her fear quickly turned to outrage, then numbing disbelief and denial, and finally a deep-seated ache of hopelessness. Over and over, she relived those dreadful moments of listening to the doctor pronounce his verdict as though he were a hanging judge. *Now* she could think of a hundred things she should have said, but she had accepted his sentence without challenge or argument. She had been simply too shocked to speak. Tomorrow she was expected to leave. She had been made to feel as if she were a neurotic woman who had made a big fuss over nothing.

The thought of going home was overshadowed by foreboding. How could she face Bill and K.C. with this news? How much more could she expect them to take? Would they believe the doctors? And what would they tell all the people who had been praying for her healing? "Sorry, folks. It's all been a dreadful mistake. They say I need a padded cell, not an operation."

An agonizing sense of failure rushed over Pann. Where should she turn for help now? Would all her doctors view her as nothing more than a hysterical female? The clinic had been her best and seemingly last hope. But, as with Dorothy in Oz, her wizard proved to be a mere mortal with no special powers to help her, and the Emerald City had turned out to be nothing more than green glass, easily shattered.

"My God, my God, why have You forsaken me?" Jesus' words on the cross echoed in Pann's heart with new and terrible meaning. She felt as though the hosts of hell were playing darts and she was the bull's-eye. Desperately she racked her brain for a Scripture to raise as a shield against the negative thoughts that assaulted her. But try as she might, she found it impossible to believe this humiliation was part of God's perfect plan and would eventually work to her good.

Dick Langford shared every ounce of his daughter's despair. In some ways, his anger and disappointment were even greater and his sense of betrayal even keener. He had felt such joy and relief at finally being able to help Pann, and now it appeared that he had only hurt her more. Finding it easier to write down his feelings than to speak them, he went to the gift shop and bought a card. On the front was a quote from Thomas Merton: "The world without storms and our lives without agony would give us nothing to grow on. Make us glad for stormy weather." Inside he wrote:

> I know you are hurt by the words of the doctors. I am angry too. I feel that I am guilty of bringing you here for such a hurt. Yet I have to believe the Lord is in it all and working for good for both you and me.
>
> The whole growth process is hard, and I believe we will grow through all this. I must claim that from the Lord for us both.
>
> You are a wonderful daughter of whom I am proud and whom I love. Dad.

Dr. Langford delivered the card along with all the encouragement and love he could muster. Then he went wearily back to his hotel room to pack and make plane reservations. Finally there was only one thing left to do. As though lifting a great weight, he picked up the telephone and placed calls to Bill and to his wife in Seattle. At the sound of Eileen's voice, he felt the hard stone of restraint in the pit of his stomach dissolve, and for the first time he broke down and wept.

XXIII

PANN DISCOVERED the letter on the plane trip home. It was among the many pages of medical reports and test results that had been returned to her upon her departure, and it bore the signature of one of the nurses who had tended her in Denver. It was surprising to find a personal letter among official medical records.

The first page briefly recounted Pann's first few days in rehabilitation and the respiratory arrest that sent her back to ICU. The second page made Pann's body tense with apprehension, and by the third page, it was clear that what she held in her hand was a six-page indictment accusing her of being an uncooperative fake. The nurse based her theory on little things she had observed Pann doing, such as hanging her foot over the side of the bed in a way the nurse did not feel was consistent with real paralysis, and on the fact that Pann seemed to respond positively to a placebo the nurse had given Pann without her knowledge or consent. Pann had developed a deep cough while she was in the hospital, and the nurse had taken it on herself to substitute flavored sugar water for Pann's prescribed medication from time to time. The nurse claimed that Pann appeared to respond as if she had taken the real medicine.

This, added to the fact that the rehabilitation therapist did not feel Pann always tried as hard as she should have, led the nurse to conclude that Pann's problems were basically functional. She expressed her opinion in terms that not only raised questions about Pann's physical condition but attacked her character as well.

As Pann shakily handed the last page to her father, she searched her memory for some clue as to why this woman disliked her so. She remembered the nurse as friendly and efficient, and try as she might, she could think of no unpleasant incident that could have motivated such a vicious personal attack. It was true that her rehabilitation nurse had accused her several times of giving up too easily. She didn't like it when Pann complained of being tired and often drove her patient to tears with her relentless pushing. Obviously the fact that she dealt with others in far worse condition had hardened her to Pann's situation.

If the therapist had written the letter, Pann would have been hurt but not entirely surprised. But the nurse who had signed the letter had always seemed pleasant and concerned. The two women had obviously conferred and passed judgment. The result was this letter, which, when added to the negative results of her initial tests, had succeeded in convincing the clinic doctors to ignore the reams of other medical evidence and conclude that Pann didn't need their help.

What motivated that nurse to step so far beyond her professional boundaries remains a mystery. But the questions her letter raised haunted Pann for the next year and a half as she tried to deal with the pain and disappointment. Her growing fear and confusion drove Pann back to Dr. Griffith, who was outraged by the treatment she had received.

"I am sick to death of doctors saying an illness must be functional just because they can't pinpoint the problem!" he fumed after hearing Pann's story. He went on to agree that some of her symptoms were functional, but certainly not the strokes themselves. He was ready to write to the clinic to strongly express his opinion.

But Pann's self-confidence had been badly shaken, and she shrank from the idea of any further confrontation. For three years she had been on a physical and emotional roller coaster, inching her way slowly and painstakingly up each incline, only to teeter precariously at the top before plunging breathlessly down the other side. The clinic experience had pushed her over the edge one more time. All Pann could do was hold on.

Things looked a little brighter in mid-July, when Pann was able to have her trach removed. But events reversed direction again in October, when she had to be carried out of church in the throes of her seventh stroke. Fortunately, it was not severe and she recovered quickly.

By early December she was home again and feeling well enough to take K.C. up to Seattle to be with her parents for Christmas. Bill flew up on Christmas Eve. He arrived with a suitcase full of presents and a cold that he promptly passed on to Pann. The cold wasted no time settling in her chest, and she ended up celebrating the arrival of 1978 from a Seattle hospital bed, barely able to breathe, much less laugh. But she managed to chuckle at the *Peanuts* cartoon her father had clipped from the paper. Charlie Brown and Peppermint Patty were having one of their famous philosophical discussions. "Years are like swimming pools, Chuck," said Patty. "We jump in one end and we splash around until we reach the other end . . . How was your year, Chuck?"

"Somebody let all the water out!" replied a dejected Charlie Brown.

"Charles Schultz must have been thinking of me when he wrote this," Pann quipped with a smile. "I'll have to write and thank him!"

Pann's breathing difficulty led to the implantation of her third and final tracheostomy tube. She hoped it would not have to be in more than ten days. It took almost ten years before it was finally removed.

The idea of a permanent trach was very hard for Pann to accept. Home again by mid-January, she followed her Seattle doctor's recommendation and began to see Dr. Paul Ward, a head-and-neck specialist at UCLA medical center who specialized in cord paralysis. Still tormented by the fear that her inability to breathe was functional, Pann arranged for Dr. Griffith to accompany her to see Dr. Ward. The idea was to have Dr. Griffith hypnotize her and then have Dr. Ward examine her cords for any sign of movement. But even under deep hypnosis, the cords remained lifeless. This experiment finally released Pann from her gnawing fears that her problem was functional.

No sooner had the question of her cord paralysis been resolved than another problem arose. Pann's constant limp and her long periods of immobility had caused the muscles in her right hip to atrophy, and the hip began slipping out of its socket. Walking became increasingly difficult and finally impossible. By April, Pann was back in the hospital for hip surgery, which, while it was successful, left her with a high fever and more fluid in her lungs. Under Dr. Eisenberg's care, Pann was tested for TB and endured a bone-marrow test. Both were negative.

On and on the roller coaster seemed to race, lurching up as Pann's fever mysteriously fell to normal, then plummetting once again as her temperature skyrocketed to a dangerous new high.

By this time, her lymph nodes were swollen and the fluid in her lungs had developed into pneumonia. During the next four weeks, tissue was taken from both Pann's lungs and liver, two extremely painful and frightening procedures that yielded no answers. Finally Dr. Eisenberg ordered Pann's lungs washed out to remove the offending fluid.

Pann: "The procedure took over two and a half hours. I was grateful that they were able to put the tube down my trach rather than my throat, but still the sensation of having my lungs flushed out with liquid was extremely uncomfortable and frightening. I remember picturing myself going up June Mountain on a ski lift, feeling the cool air and looking at the beautiful valley below. I kept myself relaxed by concentrating on every little detail, the clouds moving across the sky, the snow sparkling in the sunlight, the smell of fresh pine. Afterward Dr. Eisenberg said he had never had a patient do so well during this procedure."

The test revealed that an air-borne fungus had settled in Pann's lungs, probably by way of Pann's trach. The next day X rays showed Pann's lungs to be ninety percent clear, and she went home a few days later.

The summer of 1978 passed in blissful uneventfulness. The roller coaster had slowed to a crawl, and while she wasn't exactly going up, at least she wasn't going down. It was a good time to be with her family and to reassess where she had been and where she was going.

Pann: "I continued to see my psychiatrist, Ron Griffith, through that summer. Usually I initiated what we would talk about. I always came prepared with a list because I hated for it to get quiet. Ron said that the most interesting things came out of my mouth when I ran out of items on my list.

"We continued to deal with my anger. As a child, I had set up a pattern of not expressing anger. I never saw my dad get angry, and when my mother would get upset or yell, I resented it. I thought my mother was wrong to show her emotions so openly. Now I realize that everyone has a right to express their emotions, even anger, and that by keeping his feelings under such tight control, my dad never gave my mother the satisfaction of a good argument. Since I never saw a healthy argument as a little girl, I had no idea how to express my anger in a healthy way. When I did get upset, I would go into my closet, wrap my clothes around my head so no one would hear me, and scream.

"About this time Bill began seeing a counselor that Dr. Griffith recommended. If there is one message that Bill and I want people to hear, it is the importance of asking for help when you need it. Whether you are going through a long-term illness or some other trauma, it is vitally important to express your feelings honestly and to understand what those feelings are. Dr. Griffith used to say that we have to identify our feelings before we can properly choose how to deal with them. Until we can attach a name to those feelings, they will control us, rather than us controlling them."

The greatest setback of the summer was the gradual loss of Pann's voice. As the long, lazy days passed, she found it increasingly difficult to call K.C. in from play or to make herself heard over the drone of the television. Dr. Ward explained that her vocal cords were losing their elasticity. By the end of the summer, she was not able to manage more than a whisper, and the doctor doubted that the cords, which now hung like two stretched-out rubber bands, would ever return to normal. Pann did her best to resign herself to the raspy whisper.

About that time she also began experiencing frequent